MONICA FURLONG

With Love to the Church

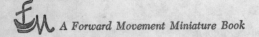

A Forward Movement Miniature Book

Foreword

MONICA FURLONG is a journalist. She compels us to read her because she is so readable. She has written about many things in many papers, but she is at her best on psychology and on religion. This is her first book. In it she brings out the difficulties which so many of us meet today in trying to be human, the psychological wounds which we have and the difficulties which may overwhelm us if, knowing our wounds, we turn to the inherited religious institutions.

Monica Furlong is a Christian. Here she says with a moving honesty why she became one. Her whole book shows why she has remained one. She has a vision of the Church as it might be. She has seen this vision embodied in the compassion and courage of some. She has been given hope that the bulk of the Church may be moving this way—because in recent British controversies, about sex and honesty to God in particular, there has been a stirring of Christian imagination and hope, as well as blind and bitter reaction. In these controversies—which have echoed round the world—mistakes were made by the radicals as well as by the reactionaries. But I share the hope which she expresses that the lasting result will be neither heresy nor reaction but a new birth of understanding and healing. I also share the hope which she mentions that through Pope John and the Second Vatican Council a new day may be dawning in the greatest church of them all. Somehow the Church which includes us will be loved into being the Church of Jesus Christ; and love involves both commitment and some words of heated truth.

Many strange things are happening in this renaissance which may turn out to be a second and better Reformation. The strangeness of the fact that I was asked to write this foreword is a trifle, but a significant trifle. I too am a publisher. My firm, which is proud to publish books by the Bishop of Woolwich and Dr. Alec Vidler (as well as books by theologians to the right), would have been glad to get hold of *With Love to the Church*. Now that Hodder and Stoughton have beaten us to it, it is a significant example of the new mood that they have charitably allowed me the opportunity to thank Monica Furlong for this book. I think that here I can speak for a whole generation, within the British churches and on their fringes. She has put our mood into words which will be remembered.

—*David L. Edwards**

* *Formerly editor SCM Press, Ltd. Currently Dean of King's College, Cambridge.*

Contents

I

Religion and the Church

LOOKING at a society like that of Britain today* one sees
a very curious sight, a community able to live neither
with Christianity nor without it. Vestigial signs of
religious belief are not hard to find; they appear in the
wish of the majority of people to have their children
baptized, or to get married, in church; they appear in
the vast sales of the Bible, in the politician's calculated
appeal to "a Christian country," and in the careful
allotting of time to religious broadcasting. When
morals, and in particular sexual morals, are being discussed it is common to hear Christianity mentioned as
if it is the basis on which our ethical life is conducted.
Speaking of someone who has behaved with excep-
tional unselfishness and goodness people will often say
he is "a real Christian," and it is very noticeable how
many people, particularly those who do not pride
themselves on moving in the tide of intellectual fashion,
like to describe themselves as Christian, even though
they may mean by this no more than "not doing anybody any harm."

* *What follows is equally applicable everywhere English is spoken.*

Yet most honest and intelligent observers would probably agree that for most people Christian belief is not a dynamic part of life. It is clear that there is a great chasm between those who retain enough wistful affection for the Church to want to maintain tenuous links with it, and those who acknowledge it as a forceful part of their everyday lives.

For most people church-going is not an essential part of life, and their chief concern is not to find a method of applying their belief to everyday life, nor do they expect to find everyday life suddenly transfigured, glistening with supernatural light. Richard Hoggart in *The Uses of Literacy* describes the working-class attitude to religion, one which is widely shared in other sections of the community:

"Ask any half dozen working-class people what they understand by religion, and very easily, but not meaninglessly, they will be likely to answer with one of these phrases: 'doing good,' 'common decency,' 'helping lame dogs,' 'being kind,' 'doing unto others as y'would be done unto,' 'we're 'ere to 'elp one another,' ''elping y'neighbour,' 'learning to know right from wrong,' 'decent living.'" He might have added the give-away phrase "not doing anybody any harm" which defines a timid, emasculated kind of Christianity, stemming more from fear and apathy than love. What has disappeared is the old sense of the creativity of religion, liberating, releasing, making men joyful, helping them to grow. Christianity appears as a tired religion, dogeared around the edges, talking in tired lauguage, shrinking from bold new thought and courageous new ideas, and, most damaging of all, seeming to have nothing to do with anything that is real in people's lives. From the great triumphs of the day in science and engineering, down to the private itching of our desires and the loneliness of our lives, we have regretfully, sometimes bitterly, come to feel that religion has nothing relevant to say.

Does it matter if belief in God gradually, or suddenly, dies in us? There are some who would regard it as a positive advantage, believing that it sets men free from a fantasy world and enables them to make a fresh start in a creative humanism. They believe that, freed from the shackles of religion, men would avoid the hideous bigotry which has inflicted such agony throughout the years. Released from watching the terrible perspectives of eternity, they would acquire a more adequate grasp of the time here available to them. They would be good without hope of reward, and without the appeal to their guilt which has been used to bludgeon them into decent behaviour hitherto.

Yet one could compile evidence to suggest that the nature of man is against them, that it is in our nature to be religious, just as it is in human nature to love, to act, to dance, to sing. Individuals may, for one reason or another, avoid these activities, certain groups may believe them so misguided or downright dangerous that they seek to discourage them, but nevertheless they assert themselves with regularity throughout human history. Man, the believer, may be as inevitable as man, the artist, using his energy fruitlessly when he tries to fight against this aspect of himself.

The question is, of course, what he comes to believe in. The humanist wants man to believe in man himself, in his abilities and potentialities. The religious man can see the nobility of this, but finds that it starves him for his essential nourishment, the brooding sense of the Other, a being different from oneself, and only partly knowable. It is striking how consistently the longing for the Other has, throughout history, broken into every kind of society, even societies such as Soviet Russia where the State strove to educate people to believe that the Other is fantasy. In a society such as our own where the paths by which, traditionally, men come to the Other, have become overgrown and blocked, there are many signs that the longing remains —in the enormous sales of the New English Bible, for example (over five million copies since 1961, of which three million are estimated to have been sold in England), or the zeal with which, a few years ago, the young flocked after an evangelist like Billy Graham. In times of fear, suffering, or at the approach of death, it is not unusual for men to turn back to the Other. Those who despise religion and see it as a canker of the personality would say that this happens because of fear, because of the primitive wish to appease angry gods; certainly this element may be present, but it is also true that after experiencing great pain or great isolation we often have the feeling that we have seen through the superficiality of our lives and perceived a great truth about the way things are.

It is this kind of experience which brings individuals back again and again to the consciousness that religion has meaning, that it is not a deception nor a neurotic adjustment but that it is a part of them which may not be denied. Those who have the experience at the deeper levels find themselves saying, like Jung, "I don't believe, I *know*." Others have known only fragments of certainty, moments which filled them with an inexplicable joy, or with a longing nostalgia, as if God had been thoroughly known once, and then lost, so creating a hunger for love which has never since been satisfied.

If the religious part of us is not, in fact, neurotic, nor a hangover from primitive fears, but something much more vital and creative, then this particular generation is unconsciously denying an important part of itself, inflicting a repression which may have results even more far-reaching than the influence of the Puritans. Like all repressions it infects and disables the imagination, and effects a poverty of religous discussion in plays, films, and books. Lame scepticism is imposed upon intellectuals with a totalitarian firmness and the imagination timidly submits to being hobbled.

Some, like Mr. Peter Brook in the following passage, reveal their passionate yearning for religion by giving themselves to what they do believe in (in this case the theatre) and then, perhaps rightly, equating the two:

11

"Such is the complete breakdown of the word that I can't make the simple statement that all great theatre is religious with the faintest hope of communicating clearly what I mean. . . . A true experience in the theatre deals with qualities and faces us with concrete realities so thrillingly above our everyday existence that we have to use a word of a different flavour to express them. Because these qualities seem to relate to human functioning at its greatest, because they transcend our normal experience, because they bring us into contact with elements that make us more alive rather than less alive, more willing to live rather than less willing to live, more willing to strive rather than less willing to strive, because they seem to draw up rather than down, I am forced to use that gothic word that also suggests a steeple pointing towards the sky. . . .

"A true experience in the theatre . . . demands an activeness from the audience as well as the stage. Any experience that is more intense than life will make an audience *want* to come back for more. An experience that is transcendental will make the audience *need* to come back. Our job must be to create addicts. . . .

"I want to see outer realism as something in endless flux with barriers and boundaries that come and go— people and situations forming and unforming before my eyes. . . . Then I want to see inner realism as another state of movement and flux—I want to sense the energies which, the deeper one goes, become stronger and clearer and more defined. . . . I want to feel the true forces that impel our false identities. . . . I want to sense what truly binds us, what truly separates us. . . . I want to hold a mirror not up to nature but up to human nature, and by this I mean that interwoven within-and-without world as we understand it in 1961—not as people defined it in 1900: I want to understand this not with my reason but with the flash of recognition that tells me it is true, because it is also in me.

"I want to see a flood of people and events that echo my inner battlefield. I want to see behind this desperate and ravishing confusion an order, a structure which will relate to my deepest and truest longing for structure and law. I want through this to find the new forms, and through the new forms the new architecture and through the new architecture the new patterns and the new rituals of the age that is swirling around us." *

A writer like John Osborne, capable of writing with a brave lack of inhibition about the wars of sex or the wounds of class, displays an almost total timidity and immaturity when exploring the religious instinct. For the entire length of *Luther* he juggles the theme, exploring its psychological and political aspects, but only at the end daring to put out a finger and touch, very tentatively, the passion which lay at the center of Luther's life. He shows Luther, in the sunset calm of his marriage and fatherhood, quoting the words of Christ, " 'A little while, and you shall see me.' Christ

_____
* *"Search for a Hunger,"* Encore, *July 1961.*

said that, my son. I hope that'll be the way of it again. I hope so. Let's hope so, eh? Let's just hope so."

In the context of the play and of the whole contemporary anti-religious mood, this seems an almost daring statement; a voice, not Luther's, speaking with the desperate gaucherie of the twentieth-century intellectual on the subject of God. The historical Luther, with all his doubts and difficulties, doubted within a framework of religious maturity which was very different.

This kind of maturity is hard to come by now and more particularly so, perhaps, in countries with a Protestant tradition. One of the few recent examples which come to mind is *The Devils* by John Whiting, a play in which Grandier, priest and sinner, comes out with a statement of religious experience which may be of profound significance for our ways of thinking and being. Grandier has sat up all night with a dying man "dirty and old and not very bright." He describes the "obscene struggle" of death and then "I came out of the house. I thought I'd walk back, air myself after the death cell. I was very tired. I could hear St. Peter's bell. . . . I walked on. They were working in the fields and called to me. . . . I could see my church in the distance. I was very proud, in a humble way. I thought of my love for the beauty of this not very beautiful place. . . . I thought of you. I remembered you as a friend. I rested. The country was stretched out. Do you know where the rivers join? I once made love there. Children came past me. . . . I watched the children go. Yes, I was very tired. I could see far beyond the point my eyes could see. Castles, cities, mountains, oceans, plains, forests—and— And then—oh, my son, my son—and then—I want to tell you—

Sewerman: Do so. Be calm.

Grandier: My son, I— Am I mad?

Sewerman: No. Quite sane. Tell me. What did you do?

Grandier: I created God!

(Silence).

Grandier: I created him from the light and the air, from the dust of the road, from the sweat of my hands, from gold, from filth, from the memory of women's faces, from great rivers, from children, from the works of man, from the past, the present, the future, and the unknown. I caused him to be from fear and despair. I gathered in everything from this mighty act, all I have known, seen, and experienced. My sin, my presumption, my vanity, my love, my hate, my lust. And last I gave myself and so made God. And he was magnificent. For he is all these things.

"I was utterly in his presence. I knelt by the road. I took out the bread and the wine. *Panem vinum in salutis consecramus hostiam.* And in this understanding he gave himself humbly and faithfully to me, as I had given myself to him.

(Silence).

Sewerman: You've found peace.

Grandier: More. I've found meaning.

Sewerman: That makes me happy.

Grandier: And, my son, I have found reason.

Sewerman: And that is sanity.

Grandier: I must go now. I must go to worship him

15

in his house, adore him in his shrine. I must go to church."

In his talking of "creating" God, Whiting cuts across orthodox theology in a single Promethean stroke that acknowledges our humanism, our post-Freudian knowledge of ourselves. When he goes on to speak of the "presence," the giving, the summons to adoration and worship, he acknowledges the Other, of which theology has spoken continually.

Though no theologian, Whiting stumbled into ideas which theologians are also reaching for. In the fruitful uncertainty of *Honest to God* which required people to look for God within themselves and their relationships, as in the writing of Tillich which it frequently echoed, we find a similar sense of "creating" God, and are plunged into the same baffling yet authentic landscape in which God both exists and does not exist, is both familar and strange, is both ourself and the Other.

But the Whitings and Robinsons are, in our society, rare and very brave exceptions. Experimenters, radical thinkers, in the realm of religion are feared and disliked by both Church and Establishment, and do not even enjoy the comfort of being intellectually fashionable. For either God is safely mummified, or else he is dangerously active, and either way it seems more comfortable to ignore him.

Working against the fear and dislike of God, however, is our powerful longing for him. This may take the form of a desperate yearning for meaning, for love, for hope, for assurance that there is more to our lives than disappointment, futility, and pain, for conviction that the joy which we experience in love, or friendship, or fellowship, is not merely the bait with which biology or society has laid the trap to make us do our duty. We want to love, we want to be loved, we want explanations for the hideous suffering that goes on in the world, we want to understand who we are and what we are doing here. If we did not want to know these things we would be less than human.

The anthropologist Malinowski, himself an agnostic, describes how he believes God to be a reality, although not a reality upon which he himself is able to act. Quoting La Place's reply to Napoleon—"Sire, God is an hypothesis of which I have never felt the need," he says, "It is the proud answer of a confident atheist, but it does not ring true to the humble agnostic. On the contrary, I should say that God is a reality and not a hypothesis, and a reality of which I am in the greatest need, though this need I cannot satisfy or fulfil. The typical rationalist says, 'I don't know and I don't care.' The tragic agnostic would rejoin: 'I cannot know but I feel a deep and passionate need of faith, of evidence, and of revelation.' Personally to me, and to those many who are like me, nothing really matters except the answer to the burning question, 'Am I going to live or shall I vanish like a bubble?' 'What is the aim, and the sense, and the issue of all this strife and suffering?' The doubt of these two questions lives in us and affects all our thoughts and feelings. Modern agnosticism is a tragic and shattering frame of mind. To dismiss agnosticism as an easy and shallow escape from the moral obligations and discipline of religion

—this is an unworthy and superficial way of dealing with it." *

How much does the Church really know or care about this kind of "tragic agnostic" or try to satisfy his hunger for faith? Barely at all, since it demands so much on her part in terms of humility, of imagination, of intellectual generosity, of compassion; in this field such flexibility is too often foreign to Christian thinking, yet it is these things which alone will meet men's suffering and need. Confronted with the spiritual impotence of the agnostic, it is of no use to apply "ought" arguments. The release can only be found by love out of imagination.

The impotence affects not only the individual, but the society of which he is a part. Malinowski describes how, in the primitive societies he observed, it was religion and religion alone which broke down men's isolation, making them part of a whole beyond themselves, binding them to their fellows.

"Religion fulfils a definite cultural function in every human society. . . . If religion is indispensable to the integration of the community, just because it satisfies spiritual needs by giving man certain truths and teaching him how to use these truths, then it is impossible to regard religion as a trickery, as an 'opiate for the masses,' as an invention of priests, capitalists, or any other servants of vested interest. . . . Religion . . . grows out of the necessities of human life. . . . The sacraments, that is, those religious acts which consecrate

* Sex, Culture and Myth, *Hart-Davis.*

the crises of human life, at birth, at puberty, at marriage, and above all at death . . . give a sense and a direction to the course of life and to the value of the personality. Religion binds the individual to the other members of his family, his clan or tribe, and it keeps him in constant relation with the spiritual world. . . . The members of a group of worshippers have natural duties towards each other. The sense of common responsibility, of reciprocal charity and goodwill, flows from the same fundamental idea and sentiment which moves clansmen, brothers, or tribesmen to common worship. . . . The conception of the Church as a big family is rooted in the very nature of religion."

Nor, in Malinowski's view, is this religion's only creative function. It is also the basis of culture. "The comparative science of religion compels us to recognize religion as the master-force of human culture. Religion makes man do the biggest things he is capable of, and it does for man what nothing else can do; it gives him peace and happiness, harmony and a sense of purpose; and it gives all this in an absolute form."

It is only now when we have travelled so far from a religious view of society that we can begin to assess how much difference it made. In *The Uses of Literacy* Richard Hoggart hinted that religion might have helped to produce the "assenting" man, a man with a generous, purposive, out-going attitude to life, who is gradually disappearing from the scene. He describes the opposite of the "assenting" man like this:

"He is infinitely cagey; he puts up so powerful a silent resistance that it can threaten to become a spiritual death, a creeping paralysis of the moral will. We hear much of the gullibility of working-class people . . . and there is plenty of evidence for its existence. But this disillusionment presents as great a danger now, and one which (it cannot be said too often) they share with other classes. Outside the personal life they will believe almost nothing consciously; the springs of assent have nearly dried up. Or worse, they will believe in the reducing and destroying things but not in assertions of positive worth; if you assume that most things are a "sell," it is easy to accept every bad charge, hard to accede to a call for praise and admiration. Some of the more powerful influences in modern society are tending to produce a generation expert at destroying by explaining-away, insulated from thinking that there is ever likely to be cause for genuine enthusiasm or a freely good act, automatically suspicious of anything not in itself disillusioned or patently self-seeking; the catch-phrase is the brittle negative 'so what?' . . . All these attitudes can feed upon themselves, and so spread to a nerve-killing effect over other areas. They can become another kind of self-indulgence, a contracting-out. There is then a loss of moral tension, a sort of release in accepting a world with little larger meaning, and living in accordance with its lack of internal demands."

Hoggart wrote these words several years before the "satire industry" had established itself; reading them, it is easy to see why satire enjoyed such a considerable popular success. Holding a few moral beliefs which liberal thought currently admired and behaving with great solemnity over these, it managed to suggest that assent was otherwise ridiculous. And without assent all creativity is doomed.

It is customary for the Church and for Christians to fire away in a hit and miss manner at contemporary morals and attitudes, repeatedly ignoring the way Christians have abrogated their responsibility and by their lack of charity, knowledge, culture, and compassion, have hastened the disintegration of society. The cold tutting over the symptoms of a sick society, the illiteracy which is intolerant of new ideas and new modes of expression, have not produced a climate in the Church in which the ice of scepticism might thaw and turn into a life-giving stream.

The purpose of this book is to try to examine some of the ways in which the churches—the Church—do reject people, do defeat the end which they exist to propogate, do make it difficult for their followers to achieve self-knowledge and the God-knowledge which lies on the far side of it. The hungry sheep look up and are not fed, and those who try to assuage their terrible hunger are frequently anathematized for the attempt.

For many sense that there is truth and meaning for them in the personality of Christ without being able to go any farther with it. The Church, the body to which it might seem sensible to turn to find out more, or where one might share one's preoccupation with others, fills so many people with feelings of dismay, or conjures a belief that it is totally irrelevant to the profound needs and longings which the person of Jesus

21

himself is able to awake in us that it has almost come to fulfil a function like that of the disciples officiously pushing away the mothers who wanted Jesus to bless their children.

For there is much to suggest that Jesus himself continues to exert a power over men. Whereas the churches occupy an ambiguous position in the community, filling people with prejudices and doubts, with apathy or with contradictory feelings of love and hate, there is a remarkable unity in people's feelings about Christ, in their sense that in his acting out of love and suffering, he touched upon the quick of their lives. His life was, in the fashionable jargon, self-authenticating; it holds together with the kind of integrity that moves us.

It may be a long journey from this kind of respect to the kind of religious faith which breathes life into a community, but then why pretend otherwise? Too much Christian propaganda in the past has tried to make a shortcut around people's reason and integrity. Asserting, rightly, that in the end it is not reason which turns a man into a Christian; believing, wrongly, that since that was truth, it did not matter how you hustled people into believing it; asserting and believing these things, the Church has been too willing to bludgeon the doubters, tempting them by their desperate longing for meaning, for personal significance, for certainty, for a firm moral code.

I write this because I think that the Church can and will change, that there are already signs of her doing so. There are, however, temptations to change in marginal ways which leave the great evils untouched, or merely substitute one kind of failure for another. It is tempting to put activity in the place of passivity, secularity in the place of ecclesiasticism, publicity and a lively interest in communications in the place of a "take it or leave it" attitude, and feel that something has been achieved. But the hungry sheep may remain as under-nourished as ever.

I do not wish to discuss the administrative changes, the re-deployment of the clergy, the new or redis-covered liturgical practices, the ecumenical movement, or any of the other reforms which are either being enacted or else are under discussion. Profound as such reforms may be in their effect, they are of less impor-tance than the huge change of heart and mind of which they are the outward form. If the change took place, then many of the reforms might occur anyway. If it doesn't take place, it won't matter whether they happen or not.

I had better make it clear what my own conception of the Church is. Within the strange, sprawling, quar-relling mass of the churches, within their stifling narrowness, their ignorance, their insensitivity, their stupidity, their fear of the senses and of truth, I per-ceive another Church, one which really is Christ at work in the world. To this Church men seem to be admitted as much by a baptism of the heart as of the body, and they know more of the intellectual charity, of vulnerability, of love, of joy, of peace, than most of the rest of us. They have learned to live with few defences and so conquered the isolation which torments us. They do not judge, especially morally; their own relationships make it possible for others to grow. It does not matter what their circumstances are, what their physical and mental limitations are. They really are free men, the prisoners who have been released and who in turn can release others.

There are more people like this in the churches than outsiders ever imagine, and meeting them is never a surprising or unnatural experience, like catching a glimpse of Stylites on his pillar. This, one knows, as soon as one has seen it, has a naturalness about it, a rightness, a sweetness that one would give anything to share. To see it is to know that this is how one ought to be, only somehow it went wrong, and one got lost instead in the muddle of worry and work, people and money.

If the Church could offer this kind of fulfilment to more people it would be doing the work of healing and preaching the gospel which is what it exists to do.

II

Why I Became a Christian

ONE of the oldest, most unattractive aspects of organized Christianity is its arrogance, its blind certainty that what it says and does is right and brooks no alternative point of view. When I became a Christian it happened because to begin with I had been moved by the charity and confidence of one priest. I had never before come upon anyone so relaxed, so unworried about religion, and I could see that out of the supreme certainty it gave him he could be more generous than most people to those who disagreed with him. There was no need to harangue people, to judge them, to needle them; God to him was a fact about life, and he proceeded to live in acknowledgment of it; a phenomenon which moved me as few things in my life have moved me.

It was a long while, however, before I could bear to consider that this individual priest was part of the Church, and the reasons for this are not far to seek. My impression of the Church ever since I could remember anything was a very different one. I remembered all those snippets in the newspapers where they quoted a sermon or article written by a reactionary vicar, all those reported statements of archbishops and bishops; in most of them one thing shone clear—a thinly-veiled distaste for people and society, and underlying the distaste a cold fear. Distaste and fear of what? Certainly distaste and fear of sex and of youth, coupled with a distrust of sheer *joie de vivre* in all its forms.

Nor has the denunciatory habit of the Church changed a great deal in the past twenty years. In order to use a thoroughly modern example, it may be interesting to examine Christian reaction to the satirical BBC program *That was the week that was*. In its hey-day the program enjoyed an audience of thirteen million and was marked by a total fearlessness of upsetting people. Thus it joked about religion, about God, about the Pope, about sex, and about perversion. No one who has ever written or talked about any of these subjects could be surprised at the amount of emotion aroused, emotion which, as always, had little bearing on anything actually said. Merely to mention these subjects is to release a flood of passionate but aimless feeling.

The program, however, took its moral stand on certain well-worn but important issues; it was against apartheid, against racialism, against hypocrisy, against hanging, against the injustice of the law on homosexuality. It seems reasonable, therefore, to have expected Christians in this country to give it a qualified approval. But with the baffling one-sidedness which so often marks Christian thinking when the conventions, and in particular the sexual conventions, are challenged, all the good things in the program mysteriously became insignificant. There was, for instance, the Bishop of Leicester, quoted in a newspaper. "It seems to be part of the policy of this program to take all things which normally command respect and reverence and make a mock of them. I do not think it says much for the people who want this form of humour or those who dispense it." Dr. Williams added that he had not seen the program.

How was it that Dr. Williams' work for the Board of Social Responsibility had not helped him to value the moral stands taken in this program? Or more fundamentally, how was it that the standards of intellectual integrity obtaining among Christians did not forbid him from judging something which he had not even bothered to see?

Then there were the 900 members of the Ilkeston Methodist Circuit who protested to the BBC "about the low moral contents and near blasphemous character of some of the items in TW3." Have the members of the Ilkeston Methodist Circuit—all 900 of them—ever protested *en masse* before? About the H-bomb perhaps, or about apartheid, or about hanging? So far as anyone knows, no. They are roused then less by the thought of human suffering and cruelty than by the remote threat of moral contamination? It would seem so.

But the privilege of demonstrating the odium which often lurks in Christian denunciations was left to the Reverend John Culey, Vicar of a church in Cheshire. Mr. Culey, finding the program not to his taste, dis-

27

covered that the principal actress in the show was "a repulsive woman with a grating voice ... generally accompanied by three or four teddy boy types with basin hair cuts." Another member of the cast was "a thick-lipped Jew boy" and the whole program was a "stark presentation of the naked spirit of our age ... what the alternative to Christianity really looks like." When the press protested at this outrageous criticism, the Vicar remarked, ominously, "The people in this parish are all pleased about what I have written."

You may object that I am being grossly unfair, since these criticisms are based largely on newspaper reports. Not only are these quite often inaccurate but they also represent a one-sided view of the Church's doings and sayings. It is news when a country vicar belches fire and brimstone in his parish magazine, but it is not news when another faithfully visits the sick, comforts the worried, and generally behaves with wisdom and love. Similarly the newspapers love it when a bishop drops a vindictive comment on modern youth, but may not choose to notice if he makes a sound, balanced speech based on reason rather than prejudice.

While I accept the unfairness with which clerical sayings are reported, I feel that there are two things worth saying about it. One is that the clergy should know perfectly well by this time that Fleet Street is waiting to pounce upon their more unguarded comments and puff them up to more than life-size; assuming that it is love and truth they care about and not getting their names into the newspapers it seems reasonable to expect them to be a little more careful in their pronouncements.

The second thing is to ask *why* the press snatches at these damaging remarks so enthusiastically. As a journalist myself I know that there is nothing Fleet Street likes better than to see people fitting neatly into the moulds already provided for them. There are a number of characters who have parts cast in the Fleet Street play. There is the film star, the model girl, the aristocrat, the politician, the housewife, the tycoon, all of whom have starring parts in the play of life. The clergyman is no exception, and like the others he must be crammed into the mould willy-nilly. And the mould, God forgive the Christians, is the mould of a narrow, frightened, sex-fearing, middle-aged bigot. This is, of course, unforgivable of the journalists, but like all such moulds, it does bear some resemblance to the facts, or it would be impossible to maintain such a fiction longer than a year or two.

For a long while now I have wondered about this image of the priest, have wondered not only where it came from but why so many of the clergy seem bent on fixing it ever more firmly in people's minds. A friend of mine who is the Vicar of a lame and frustrating country parish analyzed his own state of mind with touching honesty.

"You get so tired of the indifference, the laziness, the ignorance, that you begin to feel like Christ driving out the money-lenders in the Temple, forgetting (in your feeling of aggression) that you are not quite in the same class."

This puts a finger on exactly the right spot. The Scottish minister thundering out solemnities about the desecration of the Sabbath, the bishops grumbling on about fornication and obscene books, the archbishops holding their noses at the thought of divorce by consent (instead of adultery), reach back to a tradition which runs through Christ ejecting the money-lenders into its tap-root in the fierce utterances of the Old Testament prophets.

In all of us there is perhaps a similar temptation to make a clean sweep of the stables of our time (thus, incidentally disposing of our own uncomfortable guilt), to let rip at all the people who annoy us, to condemn the whole ridiculous boiling of them, to take the pillars of the temple as Samson did and smash everything to bits. And for much the same reason as Samson. Because our feelings of aggression and guilt are more than we can stand.

In their enthusiasm for "propheteering" many of our contemporaries ignore the fact that the Old Testament prophets did not stop at hollering curses but also provided some genuine insight into the ills of their age. It is time to question what part anger plays in the Christian life and how far, if at all, Christians are permitted to judge their neighbours and their society.

There are those—mostly to be found in pacifist bodies—who believe that anger should be rooted out of us. Those of us who do not hold this view—who believe that our anger is inextricably bound up in our humanity, that we cannot remove it even if we want to, but that if we could it would make us insipid, meaningless creatures—have the problem of distinguishing between rightful anger and the wrongful kind. And knowing that every angry man always believes, at least while he is feeling angry, that he is right to be angry, does not make the task any easier.

We may make a distinction, however, between the false prophet who merely projects his own conflict upon the world around him (and who usually gives the game away by his lack of real knowledge of what it is he condemns) and the genuine prophet whose conflict precisely *is* the struggle to understand and to heal the contemporary society. As one of the rare modern examples of true prophecy I suggest Father Huddleston's *Naught for Your Comfort*. His conflict was not in his own mind but buried truly in the sins of South African society. He was not complaining that no one loved him, but that in modern society you are constrained from loving, that is, from loving black people. There was a note of anger in his book, but it sprang, like Christ's anger in the Temple, out of the situation. It did not smack of his own private frustrations. It had no note of artificiality like the simulated anger of a father trying to frighten a small boy. It was born, as perhaps rightful anger is always born, out of a blinding certainty that this was not how things should be.

We seem to be burdened with a multiplicity of prophets, few of whom convince us that they are really battling with the problem of what love means in a society like ours. To take up one's cross daily means, I imagine, trying to be vulnerable people, trying not to put up defences and façades, trying to respond to life with love even if others misinterpret the motives. Few of us perhaps are called to be prophets, to enjoy the liberty of dictating to others; few of us have such perfect and accurate insight that our condemnations of society are in themselves healing. It seems likely that for most Christians the right course lies in gentleness, in avoiding angry condemnation of those who disagree, in working out love in terms of those we work with and live with instead of aiming vague thunderbolts at evils we have scarcely experienced.

Why then has censoriousness become such an inevitable flavour in the Christian dish? Partly no doubt because of the sense of restraint imposed by the discipline of faith. Jung and others have remarked that irritability is the price paid for goodness. It would probably be truer to say, however, that it is the price paid by those who have not really faced the nature of their own desires. Desire recognized, even if it is not satisfied, becomes a very different thing from desire repressed. One longs for Christian teaching to emphasize this openly, to impress upon Christians that it is their duty, for the sake of others as well as themselves, to admit the strength of their own desires and what the desires are, since genuine self-control begins at this point.

Christian censoriousness stems also, however, from a sense of superiority. The moral superiority rooted in class and education was well illustrated by Lord Hailsham's remark at the time of the publication of *Lady Chatterley's Lover* in a Penguin edition: "I would frankly have preferred to see it between paper boards and printed at 30s. rather than as a paperback and printed at 3s. 6d." Or in Mr. Griffith Jones' question to the jury at the Lady Chatterley trial whether it was a book they would let their wives and servants read.

There is a mixture of motives here. A feeling (one scarcely borne out by experience) that the educated and the moneyed are proof against being sexually excited by books, or that if they do become sexually excited somehow it will matter much less than if the less literate become so.

In England where historically class and literacy and faith have tended to be tangled together, this insufferable kind of superiority is carried over into religion. A letter in the *Church Times* after a television appearance by Alec Vidler in which he had been critical of the Church, lets any number of cats out of their bags.

"Those of us who are struggling to teach the young and to uphold our churchmanship in a materialist world are not helped when her ordained ministers themselves decry all that we have received and learned to hold most dear."

This correspondent clearly has an heroic fantasy of herself battling against the wicked world and dispensing the faith with a kind of Lady Bountiful sweetness. But is life like this? Is trying to be a Christian like this? In fact what makes it difficult is the fact that there is no black and white division between the materialistic world and the spiritual one. The material world is shot through with the spiritual; the Church is muddled and corrupted with material considerations. Is her real complaint against Vidler that he has scoffed at the spiritual or that he has shattered the easy and comforting simplification?

The whole Vidler controversy, and the *Honest to God* controversy which succeeded it, revealed how fundamental superiority and simplification had become to Christian thought. Alarmingly, the critics of Vidler and Robinson spent less time on the perfectly legitimate business of critics—pointing out where these writers were incorrect—than in discussing whether they had any right to say such things at all. That is to say they were less concerned in establishing the truth than in the expediency of the truth being told. One illustration of this, among innumerable others offered at the time, was the letter in the *Church Times* from the Bishop of Pontefract.

"*Honest to God* is a dangerous book likely to disturb the faith of more people than it will stimulate. It will cause a great deal of pain to faithful Christians who may not possess the Bishop's intellectual approach to theological matters." The Bishop went on to sympathize with the clergy who would have the task of dealing with those parishioners whose minds had thus been prematurely aroused. (There was an unexpected comeuppance in a later number of the *Church Times* when one of the Bishop's clerical flock claimed he would much rather deal with this sort of argument than the sort of apathy and ignorance with which he had usually to deal.)

Within a few weeks of the publication of *Honest to God* we began to hear, in Anglican discussion, frequent reference to a mythical character whom I will call "the ordinary, simple Christian." The ordinary, simple Christian had had his faith practically shattered by reading Dr. Robinson's article in *The Observer*, it seemed. (If he was that simple, though, one wonders that he read *The Observer* at all.) The ordinary, simple Christian had discovered that his Mum and Dad had not gone to heaven when they died, that heaven was not "up there," that prayers were no good, that fornication was all right; all from reading John Robinson's book. At the same time, other mythical characters also appeared on the scene (they were usually church-wardens) stoutly maintaining that they could not understand a word of *Honest to God*, that they never had believed God was "up there" anyway, and that they thought the Bishop ought to resign.

What never became clear in these discussions was the intellectual level at which John Robinson was inflicting such acute suffering, nor why at this stage of history we had suddenly decided it was necessary to depart from the sound Reformed principle that the priesthood does not exist to protect the laity from ideas.

Any layman who tries to witness to his faith in his job and among his friends well knows, in one form or another, the kind of objections to which *Honest to God* referred. Many, as the correspondence later published by the Bishop showed, found relief that someone had brought their private conflict into the open.

What many of the letters written by clergy to the

Church Times revealed, consciously or unconsciously, was a mental picture of a huge, stupid mass of laymen who could only be exposed to ideas carefully and slowly; otherwise they would be bound to get hold of the wrong end of the stick and start gleefully fornicating and neglecting their prayers as a result. The horrible contempt of the priest for the layman was revealed in criticism of the Bishop for publishing in a paperback and in ordinary language, instead of in a theological journal and in theological jargon. His real sin was that he trusted the people.

There are those, however, whose argument with the Bishop was not that he said what he said, nor that he allowed his thoughts to be published cheaply enough for the poor and the stupid to buy them, but that he said what he said as a bishop. As a bishop, they felt, he was a custodian of the faith and this should have made his duty clear. No comment should be allowed a bishop which might be in the nature of a chipping away of the faith which he was entrusted to keep. If he wanted the freedom to make the kind of comments he had made in *Honest to God*, then he should resign his office. Within his office his influence for good or evil was too great to allow him freedom of expression.

I wonder if this is not both to misunderstand how influence works for good or evil, and to misunderstand what is required from a custodian of the Christian faith. My own contention is that such people making such remarks are placing bricks in the high wall which already makes it painfully difficult for our contemporaries to see that Christianity is about love, fearlessness, and truth.

It may fairly be objected, however, that whatever errors the episcopate commits in its social comment, its real business is guarding the residuum of truth which is the bones of the Christian religion. If they are wrong-headed about the passing scene it is a pity; if they are wrong-headed about the doctrine it is a disaster.

Dr. Robinson is a difficult example of wrong-headedness because he combines, without apparently an unbearable sense of conflict, a ranging, challenging, no-holds-barred mind with a sincere orthodoxy of practice. He presents nothing as a conculsion; simply says, "This is what I am thinking at the moment, and I know lots of other people are too. Are we right or wrong?" He has none of the aggression, the dogmatism, the hysteria of the heretic. He asks with the simplicity and fearlessness of a child, but of a child who has passed through the fires of trying to apply Christian teaching in the world.

The real question is not is he right or wrong—because he has dealt more in the realm of baring new feelings, new approaches towards God than of kicking accepted truth in the face—but is he right or wrong to let others inside and oustide the Church know about the wounds in his faith, the doubts, the puzzles, the failures?

In what way, I wonder, could an action of such courage and such honesty do genuine harm? Does the fact that anyone else, even a bishop, feels no shred of doubt, help others to believe? And if it does, should faith be such an infantile process, and not something each man takes on for himself? Are we not much more likely to be strengthened in our faith and stimulated in our search for truth by being taken into the thought processes of one sensitive and intelligent man who has tried to describe what the difficulties of being a Christian are? Goodness knows, we have had enough impeccable Olympian pronouncements from bishops in the past about what being a Christian, or even being a human being, is *not* like, and their failure to have the slightest impact on our contemporaries is in exact proportion to their failure to understand what the problems are, or even that there are any problems. Yet it is obvious, both from the letters published in the *Honest to God Debate* and by talking with agnostics, that the Bishop of Woolwich *did* manage to touch many whom the churches had long failed to speak to. If a Christian and a bishop could so enter into their problems and their thoughts, then, they made it clear, the ice of agnosticism could begin to thaw. And is not this the mark of a custodian of the faith? Is it not pastorally correct to leave the ninety and nine, perhaps upsetting them in the process, while the shepherd goes in search of the lost sheep?

Yet it would be theoretically possible to find the lost sheep only to find the shepherd as lost as they. Critics of the Bishop of Woolwich suggest, with some justice, that he may have analyzed the faith to the point where nothing worth having remains.

Is this really apostasy on his part, however, or an

ability to enter into the state of mind of the agnostic and to make it his own? The only way the Church will ever begin to reach the agnostic is by simultaneously experiencing faith and unfaith; it is a hard vocation and one to which not many are called. It involves a very real sense of security and a complete trust in God. It found its perfect expression on the cross when Christ, acting with perfect obedience to God, cried that the felt forsaken. *Honest to God* (and I do not think the comparison odious) is written out of the attempt of love to embrace unlove.

What was strange was the degree of shock and fear with which it was greeted by Christians. The *Church Times* declared, inaccurately, that the Bishop had gone on public record as "apparently denying almost every fundamental doctrine of the Church in which he holds office," a remark which contrasted interestingly with the very gentle, unworried review of the book by Bishop Wand in the same issue.

What seemed missing from much of the discussion was put most admirably by Father Godfrey Pawson, the Vice-Principal of the College of the Resurrection at Mirfield: "Let us postpone (or forget) the question of episcopal propriety; let us call him John Robinson and ask whether he has helped us to know the truth. I think he has enormously." And it is this remark which too often gets left out of Christian arguments. One longs for it to be acknowledged that expediency does not matter very much, and that saving face does not matter very much, and that whether people are shocked and upset does not matter very much, but that truth

39

does. It is more important that the "ordinary, simple Christian" should be exposed to truth than that he should bumble on in spiritual cotton-wool. It is more important that we should know what the contemporary situation really is, as a result of the sharp exchanges promoted by Robinson's book, than that the Church of England should suffer the scandal of a recalcitrant bishop.

What so many of our arguments unconsciously reveal is a fear of the truth, or rather a fear that if the truth were known, Christianity would cease to exist. What we owe to God, if he is the God we claim to worship, is the acknowledgement that we have nothing to fear either in ourselves, or in the "simple faithful." It will take more than a bishop to do it substantial harm; the truth has a way of asserting itself with an undeniable insistence.

What is lacking, and has been throughout Christian history, is the urbanity, the confidence, the sophistication (to use the word in its modern, inaccurate sense) of a Gamaliel. There is an arrogance in many Christians which insists that God cannot get along without our fervid championship and that, therefore, we must constantly be leaping to his defence. We see the horrid spectre of either heresy or indifferentism looming in the twilight, and the zeal stands out on our forehead like drops of sweat. In this mood the Christians hunted down the heretic, persecuted the Jew, dragooned the believer, hunted the witch, fought the Turk, embarked on wars against one another. It has been the supreme tragedy of the Church. And we cannot pretend that in recent controversies—with Robinson, Vidler, and others—the old acrid smell of the heresy hunt has been entirely missing.

Yet Gamaliel put the Sanhedrin right on all this in the first century, thus incidentally saving the Church from extinction almost before it had got going.

"Refrain from these men and let them alone: for if this counsel or this work be of man, it will come to nought:

"But if it be of God, ye cannot overthrow it; lest haply ye be found even to fight against God."

The sad thing is that just as a man who is convinced he will die of cancer usually gets carried off by something different though it may be equally nasty, so while Christians worry ceaselessly about preserving the doctrine, and about indifferentism, a quite different and perhaps more terrible apathy creeps up on them unbeknown.

It seems to me that *The Representative*—provided one regards it as a criticism of Christians in general, and not the Roman Catholic church in particular—illustrated this particularly well. Writing about it in *Prism* Nicholas Mosley said this—"*The Representative* is about . . . the failure to imagine the meaning, the appalling evil, of the murder of the Jews. But as the satanic doctor points out in the last scene, the Church is an old hand at not facing this. The Church, in fact, was responsible for burning 350,000 heretics in Spain (and *alive*, the doctor adds). Throughout the play (this is seen better in the published and longer version) there is the correlation between the Church dignitaries and the Nazis—they are both seen as people who have given themselves over to something impersonal. They both dress up, strut, use a lot of ritual; they both think that just because a man holds some position he cannot be wrong (Hitler, the Pope); they both project their own responsibility on to this sort of man (thus rendering him impersonal) and empty themselves of humanity. And thus they all become, naturally, devils or easy meat for the devil—as the Bible tells us.

"It is after seeing a play like this, and asking—what is wrong with these people? that I think one sees the point of, for instance, Harry Williams's vision of the Church as in one sense a huge mechanism for keeping people from the truth. And then one is faced with the sort of answer that Harry Williams suggests—some courageous effort at spontaneity, some abandonment to experience, in order to become a human being again, in order to *feel*. That this is difficult language and risky, is obvious. But if anyone can think of anything better, let him. The point is that this huge sort of evil is going on all the time; and most Church people can't imagine it, can't make any sort of contact with it. So let someone, at least, have a try. But do not let anyone, for goodness sake, go on about more prayer and fasting. The Pope, and all the other dignitaries of *The Representative,* did that."

Yet as fast as a few Christians try to record their sense of what Mosley elsewhere calls the "deadness, madness, lack of connection" in the Church, there are others urging that more rigidity, more conformity and less sensitivity is the answer.

One saw this with disturbing clarity in *The Christian Mind* by Harry Blamires which was acclaimed in some Christian circles and more especially by Dr. Mascall who described it as "the most important religious book of a nontechnical kind that has appeared in the last ten years." One hopes not the most significant.

Blamires's contention is that we should develop something he calls "the Christian mind," a way of thinking and talking in opposition to the secular mind. His book is marked with arbitrary, withering judgments of contemporary figures—John Osborne has not great talent, he says, and his fame "will be ephemeral." Henry Miller goes in for "rabid obscenities" but in spite of this is a rebel of the right type. D. H. Lawrence evokes the wince-making statement that "The educated man who can read *Lady Chatterley's Lover* and not rock with laughter has a sick mind." But his brutal, Philistine judgments matter less than the suggestion of brutality, the old hint of prophetic aggression in the way he wants Christians to assert themselves. He writes about the terrible and shameful history of Christian fanaticism like this: "No men more loudly and impressively than the officers of the Holy Inquisition claimed that temporal well-being must be subordinated to eternal well-being; that physical pain and earthly suffering were as nothing when weighed in the balance against the damnation of a soul. One might go further and say that no body of men more strenuously strove to preserve the distinctness and distinctiveness of the Christian mind. *We have perhaps been frightened too much by horrors of that kind."* (The italics are mine.) Too much? Can we ever be frightened too much? At least one of the things that keeps the agnostic from the Church today is the knowledge that men can behave like monsters while proclaiming the God of love. Through terrible centuries men talked of Christ while they burned the heretic and hunted the Jew. Mr. Blamires objects that the secular world does not hear the Christians speak with a sufficiently distinctive voice. But is not the trouble that it has heard the Christian voice speak all too clearly in the past, and hears echoes of that determined intolerance in clerical pronouncements to this day? Rightly the secular world determines that this is not the healing it needs for its admitted disease.

It seems to me to be the strength of Robinson, Williams, Vidler, and the rest, that they have finally rejected the prophetic righteousness, the cocksure certainty so often inflicted upon the world. They have chosen, instead of emphasizing the differences between the Church and the world, to show how they are inextricably bound together. In the heart of secularity Christ is there to be found. In the heart of the Church, secularity, often of a corrupt and loveless kind, is to be found.

The admission by such writers of the guilt of the Church brings down upon them the charge of disloyalty. When Vidler remarks that "there's been so much suppression of real, deep thought and intellect, alertness and integrity in the Church," I believe that many Christians and certainly many non-Christians believe him to be right. Yet the habit of pretending that all is well is too strong; the *Church Times* and its correspondents leap automatically to the defence, protesting far too much. It is far easier to keep to the well-worn Christian habit of projecting our own wickedness outwards upon the world.

Dr. Robinson and the others have refused to do this, however. Mr. Williams, in particular, has concerned himself with the way guilt operates within the Church and upon individual Christians. I believe each of these writers reveals the pattern which psychiatrists note in people who have at last faced their problems. There is a lack of defensiveness, of nervous tension, of disturbing aggression. In contrast to them, other contemporary Christian writers suddenly appear evasive, superior, condescending. We have wondered for years why Christians could not communicate successfully with intelligent contemporaries. The reason now becomes apparent, and the writers who *have* faced and admitted the Church's guilt have found it possible to communicate with remarkable ease.

A new approach to the scepticism of our age has been shown to us. So long as we thunder like the prophets out of our own unadmitted aggression then others will, quite properly, take no notice of us. And so long as we are more concerned with face-saving or in plying the "correct" answers than with truth, then they will recognize us for the humbugs and hypocrites we often are. The only real antidote to scepticism is love and truth; it is the kind of healing the Church is there to provide.

III

About Sex

IF anxiety is a noticeable reaction of many Christians when their doctrines are questioned, the response when the Christian sex ethic is questioned is sheer panic. Nowhere is the gay fearlessness of the early Church less apparent than in the desperate leading articles about sex in religious newspapers or in the flurry of furious correspondence received by any journalist or writer who dares even to enter the current discussion.

Let us for the moment leave out of the argument the question of whether what some or all of the writers said was right or wrong. What I am concerned with is the extraordinary violence of the response to their remarks. Since the actual words used by the people concerned long since got lost sight of in the welter of abuse, it may perhaps be worth considering what was said over again and trying to understand why Christians felt so strongly.

What the Bishop of Woolwich actually said when giving evidence at the Lady Chatterley trial was this: "Clearly, Lawrence did not have a Christian valuation of sex, and the kind of sexual relationship depicted in this book is not one that I would necessarily regard as ideal, but what I think is clear is that what Lawrence is trying to do is to portray the sex relationship as something essentially sacred." He went on to quote Archbishop William Temple, "Christians do not make jokes about sex for the same reason that they do not make jokes about Holy Communion, not because it is sordid, but because it is sacred." Dr. Robinson continued, "I think Lawrence tried to portray this relation as in a real sense something sacred, as in a real sense an act of holy communion."

In the weeks that followed he was attacked on many different levels, from bishops down to volumes of letters from ordinary Christians.

Professor Carstairs said this: "*Is* chasity the supreme moral virtue? In our religious traditions the essence of morality has sometimes appeared to consist of sexual restraint. But this was not emphasized in Christ's own teaching. For him the cardinal virtue was charity, that is consideration of and concern for other people. . . ." *

What Dr. Henderson said, to a seminar of teachers which he believed to be conducted in private, was: "I do not myself consider that a young man and woman who plan to marry and who have sexual intercourse before their marriage are unchaste. I simply cannot convince myself that they are immoral."

It would take too long to go into *Towards a Quaker View of Sex*, which, I think, declares itself basically in favour of chastity and fidelity. The Quaker Report

* BBC Reith Lectures, 1962. Published as This Island Now (Hogarth Press).

advocated a new approach to the homosexual, one which would free him (or her) from the crippling burden of having to conceal his own nature even from his friends as well as from the terrors of blackmail or imprisonment.

What was striking about the Christian response to all these statements was its forcefulness. Some of the speakers were Christians, and all of them showed sympathy to the Christian point of view. All put their point of view humbly and tentatively, not claiming certainly that they were in the right, but rather indulging in what John Robinson described as "thinking aloud." Yet the vigour of the Christian opposition suggested not so much that their ideas were wrong, but that it was wrong of them even to question the correctness of Christian morality. Christian morals, they suggested, were such a delicate plant that if the wind of controversy merely blew upon them they might wither and die. Sir Cyril Black, speaking in the House of Commons, quoted Dr. Ernest Claxton, the Assistant Secretary of the British Medical Association. "As a doctor and official of the British Medical Association I can tell you that extra and premarital intercourse is medically dangerous, morally degrading, and nationally destructive."

Men like Sir Cyril hold rigidly to the point of view that society rests upon chastity as upon a foundation. For them chastity represents security—take it away and society would crumble to bits.

One longs for them to recognize that the argument about national greatness is an unChristian one; God is not an instrument for the glorification of the State. One longs for them to defend Christian sexual morality purely on the grounds that it is the most perfect expression of love.

For too many, both inside and outside the Church, Christian morals appear to represent a safeguard against the force of their own desires. They are appalled by the violence of them, aware of the pain and distress they could easily cause to others, afraid of the condemnation of society which an unbridled sexual appetite incurs, and they feel that to save themselves they must crush their longings with something even more powerful. The steamroller which, tragically, they choose is the Christian faith. Having been merciless on themselves, however, they become merciless upon others. Envy and contempt mingle horribly in their consideration of the deviant or the indulgent. Their fantasies of those unable, for one reason or another, to achieve the Christian sexual ethic, make it impossible for them to assess them accurately, or to look gently and wisely upon those whose conduct or emotions differ from their own. For to do so would be to run the risk of suffering their own agonies over again.

There is also another strain in Christian thinking and talking about sexual matters which reaches back far into church history. The Bishop of Woolwich, describing the response to his remarks about the sacredness of sexual intercourse at the Lady Chatterley trial, commented—"Only too many of the letters I have received reveal that otherwise devout and moral persons still think that sex is disgusting, and that any book which portrays the sexual relationship is, *ipso facto*, undesirable. But this is not the Christian view." Others who have written about sex, from however moral a standpoint, will share the Bishop's view. It is one of the ironies of journalism that articles dealing frankly with sexual subjects evoke letters of a terrifying ferocity and sometimes obscenity from readers defending purity.

What faces us here is not only the failure of individuals to recognize their own nature, but also the extent to which the Church has encouraged the dichotomy between the spirit and the senses and set the seal of approval upon it. Most women who are practicing Christians will at some time in their lives have felt the anti-feminist bias of the Church, a bias which still reveals itself in the way the Church undervalues, underpays, and underworks the women who offer it their services. Anti-feminism is only one way, however, in which Christianity has exhibited a fear of the sexual impulse.

Historically the Church set an exaggerated value on chastity by a perverse asceticism which insisted that the spirit must be cultivated at the expense of the body and the senses. The great opportunity to persuade men and women to rejoice in their sexual powers and to make them part of the love-song which is supposed to be the Christian life upon earth was squandered.

The evident perversity of so much Christian teaching about sex in the past has now made any Christian statement on the subject suspect.

Nor is fear of talking openly and plainly about sex

51

the only way in which Christians offend their contemporaries. They do so also by their superiority, their
conviction that they and they alone practice decent
standards. Much as some would like to believe it, a
sense of responsibility is not confined to church-goers.

A friend of mine who was until recently a profes-
sional soldier told me of the valiant efforts of some of
his married men not to be unfaithful to their wives
during long absences from home. He described one
occasion when his battalion arrived at a town famed for
its pretty and clever prostitutes after long weeks of
fighting, and how some of its members refused to go
out after dark at all, partly, he felt, because they knew
if they did so they would betray their wives, partly
because prostitutes, however much men boasted of
their charms afterwards, were invariably a disappointment, leaving a sense of being cheated of the real thing.
There were also, of course, many who willingly accepted the substitute for love, but it was worth noticing that, without the help of Christian insights,
some would not have anything but the real thing, sens-
ing for themselves that this was a step towards madness, loneliness, and disconnection.

In a certain kind of clerical mythology, however,
men and women have no such wisdom, no such instinct
to get their relationships right if they possibly can.
Yet responsibility crops up consistently in all sorts of
places. This, for instance, was the *Daily Sketch* on
the morning after the Lady Chatterley verdict was
declared:

"The Old Bailey judge and jury have not taken decisions for any of us as parents. They have forced each one of us to make a choice whether or not we wish our children to buy sexual descriptions at pocket-money prices. In that sense only are we a more responsible society this morning. But this responsibility is something we now have to exercise for ourselves, instead of being able to hide behind a verdict that would have done it for us."

It is when you read a statement like this in a newspaper not usually noted for its maturity and wisdom that you begin to see the point of Bonhoeffer's remark about man having "come of age." For the mark of an adult is not that he is necessarily sensible or controlled all the time, but that he knows he is someone who is held responsible for his own actions and that, in the slang phrase, no one else will "carry the can" for him.

To the *Daily Sketch*, it was evident that people knew enough of their own natures and cared enough about their children to think the matter out for themselves.

What is deeply disturbing about many hierarchical utterances about sex is their superficiality, their unwillingness to suggest that our ability to love joyfully, and with a proper degree of self-control, is impaired far less by books and films and lewd advertisements than by more fundamental experiences. It is a commonplace for clerics to talk about Christian homes, but almost unheard-of for them to mention the "stumbling blocks" within family life which may preclude the possibility of mature loving relationships. I cannot remember any priest warning fathers against harshness with their children, or mothers against possessiveness or excessive domination. Yet it is within the family that the child develops its attitude to the other sex and towards forming loving relationships in general.

Because of coldness or misplaced emotion within the family too many grow up lacking in the confidence to love others effectively; here is the breeding-ground for divorce, for many pathetic deviations, and for intolerably painful loneliness. Is it not time that archbishops and bishops knew where the springs of human behaviour lie, and did not pretend that corruption lies within books or plays, which are but the symptom of our bewilderment?

And why do they pretend? Partly because to set sin within a context of family environment diminishes people's responsibility for what they do. If you once admit, for example, that a whole range of sexual misbehaviour stems not from devilment in the individual or from the general wickedness of the times, but from a fear of women which originated with a man's mother, then what you seem to have said is that the individual has no free will. And any archbishop would have proper inhibitions about saying that.

But if he genuinely were to care more about releasing the man from his suffering than proving doctrinal points, he would soon discover that freewill operates in the realm of the man facing the nature of his compulsions so that whereas he was completely subject to them, he may eventually achieve freedom from them. Which is precisely the sort of miracle that Christianity is about.

What is especially frightening to many both outside and inside the Church is that far from encouraging those who come to them to face their problems, many clergy show small sign of having dared to face their own. The clergyman, like the psychiatrist, needs to know a great deal about the darker side of his own nature if he is to acquire enough freedom to see other people's problems in their true light. If he does not understand himself then he is bound to be the prey of anger, of censoriousness, of fear, or of morbid fascination when confronted with behaviour or even ideas which appear to transgress his code.

It does not in the least matter how grave or disabling his private problems may be, but it matters very much how far he pretends, even to himself, that his beliefs automatically destine him to a state of health.

It is, however, so much less painful to project one's disappointment and failure outwards and to curse the times. The more fearful people are of the forces within them, the more fearful they are of anything in society which may uncover their longing. And the more repressed any given society, the more it seeks to control what others do or even think. An example of this is Eire where the Church, growing ever more fearful of modern influences, encourages wholesale banning of newspapers and books.

However much the "ordinary man" in Ireland, or anywhere else, may childishly submit to this kind of interference with his intellectual liberty (and I believe he knows condescension perfectly well when he sees it), this kind of fearfulness brings Christians ever more under the contempt of intelligent people who are accustomed to think for themselves. Quite properly they do not think that priests have any right (or even are particularly well-endowed) to decide what books they may read, and their knowledge of psychology is sufficiently sophisticated to tell them exactly what the Christians are trying to hide.

Since the clergy rarely admit, either publicly or privately, to having problems of their own, intelligent observers are left with an impression of a body which seeks to organize the moral stakes without being honest enough to declare its own interest.

There are moving exceptions who make us intensely aware of how far the others fall short. Even in Ireland there are priests like the Jesuits Father Connolly of Maynooth and Father John Kelly. Peter Lennon, writing in *The Guardian,* remarked of Father Kelly, "he can take a film like *L'Avventura* and share his experience of this fine description of desolation and isolation in love without a trace of any 'clerical' attitude. We feel that we can have complete confidence in his intellectual honesty." We can sense, and share, Mr. Lennon's gratitude for a priest who had no axe to grind save the axe of truth.

A priesthood which cares only for truth needs to have less encouragement to protect the flock—the flock, even in Ireland, is no longer an illiterate peasant community which can only be allowed ideas in tiny, digestible sips—and much more encouragement to expose people to more difficult kinds of thinking, more strenuous forms of culture, and more compassionate forms of loving.

Since the truth hurts, and since learning may be a painful process, this will inevitably involve the Church in scandal and unpopularity. There are many laymen (and even some agnostics) who are all too grateful for the blind condemnations of the Church, and who will join with louder voices than the clergy in blanket condemnations of the "new morality" and the "new theology" without trying to understand what it is they condemn. It is time Christians admitted that this is a defence—against thinking, feeling, and understanding.

Christian double think was never better illustrated than in the joint statement of the churches on divorce —revealingly the only joint statement on any subject at all which the denominations have so far achieved together. The statement was provoked by Mr. Leo Abse's Matrimonial Causes and Reconciliation Bill but was only really concerned with one clause in it, that which allowed divorce after seven years' separation, whether or no a matrimonial offence had been committed against the petitioner. "Until now," ran the Statement, "laws of marriage in this country have been framed on the assumption that marriage is a lifelong covenant not to be terminated solely by the wish of the partners: Mr. Abse's Bill would change that by allowing divorce by consent of the partners. It is said that at present when marriages have broken down there is often recourse to a fictitious planning of matrimonial offences in order that a divorce may be obtained. But we believe none the less that it would help to undermine the basic understanding of marriage as a lifelong union if the principle were introduced that a marriage could be terminated by the desire of the partners to terminate it. . . . We think that there would be an increasing tendency to enter upon this covenant less seriously if the law allowed it to be ended on the principle of the partners' own desire to end it. . . . We must have great sympathy with those whose marriages have come to grief, and with the children of people living together outside wedlock. We must also care for both the partners and the children of a marriage."

What is immediately striking about this document is that it sounds intolerably conceited. The writers of it genuinely believe that it is they and they alone who are preserving the meaningfulness of marriage, that if they let go for one single moment disaster will come rushing down. This finger-in-the-dyke complex is noticeable in many Christian utterances, and it is strange that the speakers never appear to notice how little others are taken in by their heroic pose. For as a matter of simple fact, Christians did not discover marriage, and the institution has flourished quite as successfully within other cultures and other faiths.

More seriously we can observe once again the "Daddy knows best" note of patronism, the suggestion that "ordinary" people could not possibly be allowed to decide when their marriage had become unbearable and that therefore authority must hold all the strings.

But, of course, like anyone accustomed to being manipulated by authority, "ordinary" people long ago learned how to twist its tail. It is not merely "said" that there is often recourse to a fictitious planning of matrimonial offences in order that a divorce may be obtained. It actually happens. I could, without undue effort, name a dozen couples I can think of who pretended to commit adultery in order to obtain a divorce, although their marriage had, in fact, become intolerable for quite other reasons.

Can the Christian conscience really connive at this kind of deceit, believing that it is preferable to a seven years' wait and then a divorce in which no lies are needed? Are not the pious phrases of the statement concealing a deplorable cynicism?

But above all, the statement smacks of cowardice and evasion. It has neither the nerve to come out squarely against divorce in the central Christian tradition, saying uncompromisingly that Christianity is about loving your enemy even when he happens to be the man you are married to, nor to allow its rock-like attitude to be broken by compassion for the secularism of many who live under our marriage laws.

What it lacks is any sign of genuinely caring, of really trying to understand and to bear the suffering of, say, a woman whose husband turns out to be a paranoic or a psychopath, of the man whose wife is incurably frigid, of the many couples who go trustingly and lovingly into marriage only to discover later that one of them is too immature or too neurotic or too inverted to build a viable marriage at all.

The Church offers such couples the ludicrous alternative of continuing in a living hell or of putting on the degrading charade of adultery.* And the reason it offers for officially backing the first alternative is that "it upholds the Christian meaning of marriage." By this is meant that if one sheep strays the rest will follow. It seems to be doubtful that marriage failure works in this way. Most people have too much at stake, emotionally, pridefully, even financially, to want to destroy their marriage for no reason at all. And nearly all of us want very badly to make a success of our close relationships, even the sort of people who usually do end up making a mess of them. Successful or unsuccessful, we all want to love and be loved. To suggest that a couple might fling into marriage without giving it a thought if they knew they could get out of it seven years later suggests a wilful ignorance of the ardour young people bring to their love life. There *are* people, of course, who are irresponsible in their relationships and in the wounds they inflict. But then under the present laws they would wriggle out of marriage in a great deal less than seven years.

What we need from the Church in the field of divorce is a great act of courage, a frank statement that the Bible's teaching on divorce is vague and contradictory, and that it was, in any case, framed at a time when the status of women was so different as to make marriage virtually a different relationship altogether. The Church should make it plain to her children that there are relationships when love makes it imperative for a marriage to continue, and others when

---

* In the Episcopal Church there are certain other "reasons" which enable a bishop to declare a marriage annulled.

it is braver and better not to go on since we may damage our partners and they us. Is not this a more honourable method than the backstairs workings of the Sacred Rota, mysteriously making illicit relationships of celebrated Roman Catholics licit, or the queer farce in the Church of England whereby people remarrying after divorce are gently tutted after and then welcomed back once they have safely done their marrying somewhere else? Excommunication would be more honest. The admission that marriage has become impossible would be truer to life and love.

It is hard for Christians to accept that people can fly in the face of their teaching and achieve a positive good. So they get into the habit of talking as if divorce must lead to unhappiness. But divorce does not always lead to greater unhappiness. I can think of divorces where not merely one but both of the partners have achieved a happiness and fulfilment that they could never have achieved with the first partner.

If Christians are to be listened to they must drop the emphasis on fear, which is so often not justified by the facts, and beg and beseech men and women to think instead in terms of unselfish love. For fear quite evidently does not stop girls conceiving unwanted babies, women having back-street abortions, young people getting venereal disease, or married couples being unfaithful to one another. But unselfish love could make an enormous difference to all of these things.

IV

The Secular World

AT the heart of the Christian's difficulties at the moment lies his relation to the secular world. It has, of course, always been a problem. In the early centuries of the Church it seemed right and proper to strengthen the fellowship, and within it to find courage to bear the pressures of the world. After the Concordat with Constantine the world invaded the fellowship, claiming it for its own. In the centuries that followed, state after state and monarch after monarch boasted of Christian allegiance, sometimes using Christ as an excuse for aggression, sometimes pursuing Christian worship and expediency simultaneously, like Henry VIII who could hear Katharine Howard's screams for mercy while he knelt placidly at prayer in his chapel.

Within the Church and within its denominations there have always been sects and sub-sects whose tendency was to withdraw from the world and its wickedness and to lead a life of separateness. There has also, again and again, been an outward-looking movement which took as its text the injunction to go and preach the gospel to every creature. At its worst the tendency to withdrawal represented neurosis, the disability which encourages people to restrict their relationships within limits which will protect them from the dangers of self-exposure. At *its* worst, the tendency to go out into the world and preach the gospel to every creature, represented a will to impose oneself upon others, a lack of respect for their individuality and identity. One thinks of the kind of missionary who had a mania for getting the savage decently covered.

There have also been many sinister combinations of Christian extraversion and introversion. I can think of an evangelist of our own day who does his best to preach the gospel to every creature, but preaches an alarmingly introverted gospel which clings inflexibly to a primitive conception of heaven and hell, and never dares to face the complexities of scientific or psychological thought. He does, of course, as any popular preacher must, put on the appearance of being a modern figure, mention modern situations, use the apparatus of modern propaganda. But this is a long way from exposing oneself to the real dilemmas of modern thought, from entering into the lonely and frightening regions travelled by, say, Jung or Teilhard de Chardin or the physicists. Or alternatively to exploring the modern situation through writers, painters, playwrights. It costs a Christian more to read Hochhuth, to read Hannah Arendt, to read Beckett, Mailer, Pinter, to look at Guernica, and *then* to tot up the cost of behaving like Christ in contemporary society, than to make a "decision" in an emotional whirl and a mental vacuum.

But my point for the moment is to say how easily,

how wickedly easily, Christians turn from love to the most arrant kinds of self-seeking. It happens in the tiniest sects, it happens in the great monolith of Roman Catholicism, it happens through all the shades in between. Neither the inner light, nor authority, neither scripture nor tradition, neither unorthodoxy nor orthodoxy, can overcome this subtle and disturbing form of corruption.

It happens, of course, precisely because Christians are *not* separate, but are very much part of the world. Such experiences as baptism, a blinding awareness of the love of God, a passion for love, may and do produce profound changes in the personality, but fears, limitations, the sort of childhood suffering which gives a bias towards sin are still there.

It is a real temptation in this situation to reject the world in an attempt to reject the most unsavoury parts of our own personality. The sensualist has a temptation to become the ascetic, the masochist to embrace an elaborate penitence, the sexually-obsessed to become harshly critical of others' sexual conduct. This is so much less painful than facing our own sickness and our own sin. Yet it was, I believe, about this kind of emptiness, this kind of poverty of spirit, that Christ was talking in the Beatitudes. Blessed are they who have no illusion about themselves; it will be easier for them to see other people as they are.

Christians are a long way from admitting this kind of identity with the world. The pronouncements about teen-agers, about the "ordinary man," about non-church-goers, about divorcees, seem a long way from admitting that the Christian is in no way superior. Christians may regard themselves as "miserable sinners" in the litany, but their actions suggest a very different point of view.

What is odd is that Christians rarely define what they mean by the world. Many biblical texts, as well as the baptismal service in the Book of Common Prayer, suggest that it is something pretty disreputable that we should do well to avoid, but they never make it entirely clear what it is. The more puritanical writers and thinkers have chosen to identify the world with sexual emotion, and with the colour and gaiety and spontaneity and enjoyment which spring from the senses. They set out to claim that the world is lust and selfishness and greed, which is not necessarily a bad definition, but they actually seem to be saying something else—that it is pretty girls, virile young men, the act of love, the pleasure of eating and drinking, behaving with lack of inhibition. And if Christians are rejecting this, then they are running curiously counter to the world as God has made it, and to men and women as he has made them.

Or one might define the world rather differently, somewhat as Christ himself seems to have defined it. Christ often spoke of "this world" or "this life," suggesting that it was those who could only see things in terms of "this life" who lost their way and denied truth. If you thought only of "this life," he seems to say, then you could not see that there was anything more important than comfort, wealth, sensual gratification, power, fame, and gradually you came to live for one or another of these things. This was to build your house upon sand, since eventually you discovered that pursued as ends in themselves these things were no good and only made you more alone and more unhappy.

The meaning and beauty of life came from acknowledging another dimension, the dimension of God. Within this dimension was another range of thinking and feeling, the range of love, of forgiveness, of self-knowledge and the knowledge of others. It was only through plunging into this other dimension that men could overcome their isolation and reach one another. It was only because of it that "the world" had any reality at all.

Now Christians have long maintained that their faith contained the only reality, and they have frequently suggested, I think mistakenly, that the proper attitude to "the world" is contempt, tempered with a fear of its power. We have seen with what ease contempt for "the world" changes into contempt for the people in it who do not perceive the other dimension. Yet when the Christian moves outside the dimension of love in his attitude to other people he is as much of "this world" as they are.

The hopeful thing about some of the most enlightened post-war Christian thinking is that it has begun to hammer out a new way of regarding "this world." In the words of one young theologian I know, "We used, with sublime arrogance, to talk of 'taking Christ to Africa or to China,' just as if Christ was not already there." Christ was already in China or Africa long before a single missionary set foot there. Christ was part of the structure of other faiths, of other cultures, of art, of family and social life, of the individual's thinking and feeling. The gospel, the "good news," consisted in encouraging men to make a discovery—that the instinct within them which they had known all their lives and which had been continually frustrated—the impulse towards vulnerability, towards love, towards freedom—was a true instinct, an instinct which originated in the principle of life itself. Again and again, the European Christian exaggerated the alien quality of the more primitive people to whom he preached Christianity, perhaps in an unconscious attempt at self-protection against the impact of a primitive society upon himself. While he talked of reconciliation, of men being brothers, he etched the dividing lines more and more deeply. The black man might become a Christian, but at a terrible price. The price he must pay was to be isolated from his pagan culture and to become an imitation white man. Only thus could the distinctive quality of Christianity survive.

This is a pattern which, with variations, has been repeated over and over again in Christian history. Christian relations with Judaism have been marked with a similar attempt to emphasize the differences rather than the similarities. In the early days of the Church there was some reason for this. Jewish persecution of the Christians, together with the need of the young Church to cut itself free from Jewish legalism, enforced separation. By medieval times, in many parts of Europe, the Jew was not simply a man who did not accept the sonship and kingliness of Jesus Christ; he had become a threat merely by the fact of not be-lieving, and must be humiliated, hurt, and driven out. Christian contempt branded the Jew as a menacing figure, and it was by playing upon this old, irrational fear that Hitler persuaded his nation that it was neces-sary to murder millions of men, women, and children.

Yet the Christian attitude to the Jew has only demon-strated in an extreme form the feeling of fear and hatred engendered by the unbeliever. Since the Jew explicitly disbelieves that Christ is the Word made flesh then the sanctions against him have been more deliberate and more violent. Yet the same lack of love, the same inability to see Christ in the other, and to reverence him, is evident in the Christian attitude to those who flout their ethical beliefs or deny their faith.

The reason is still fear. What is lacking, what the early Church so impressively seems to have had, is the kind of fearlessness which could allow men to ex-plore people and ideas and experiences very different from what they were used to, blissfully confident that they would find Christ there just as surely as they had found him in the garden or on the road to Emmaus. Without this confidence Christians become as narrow, as intolerant, as cruel, as the Marxists, less concerned about truth than in trotting out the approved answers.

When the Christian abandons his nervousness and seeks instead after truth and love, then his world opens out most wonderfully. His relations with the atheist, the agnostic, the Jew, need no longer be cramped by awkwardness or intolerance. For all of these, if they are good men and brave men, are trying to speak a language which is also common to the Christian, the language of truth.

Yet it is not only fear that has divided Christians from others, but also the knowledge of a different danger—the danger of indifferentism. To the indifferentist all cats are grey, all believers as good as all other believers. The indifferentist is essentially a sentimentalist, who neglects the fierce exactions of love and truth, and believes that all that matters is "goodwill." The only body of believers he recognizes is "all men of goodwill."

The Christian cannot pretend that he believes in nothing distinctive, nor that his beliefs about the existence and the nature of God are unimportant. The more he trusts his beliefs and lives by them, the more distinguished, and the more obviously different will he become. He cannot deny that he believes in the uniqueness of Christ, not even as an act of love towards others who cannot believe it too. Having properly examined and questioned his belief and tested it as thoroughly as he is able, he is left with a solid residuum that he cannot deny. It seems to me dishonest for Christians to talk of being themselves agnostic, as if they meant by this what the agnostic means by it. The consequence of belief cannot be thus escaped.

If the Christian cannot deny what he believes to be the truth, however, he can be infinitely less condescending and more humble in his approaches to others. It seems to me wrong for him to adopt a fiercely militant approach to the unbeliever, wrong for him to play upon others' sense of guilt, wrong for him to talk of "strategy" as if conversion were a sales campaign or a political manoeuvre. It is wrong because it shows no reverence for the personality of the unbeliever, no acknowledgment that he may have reasons—intellectual or psychological—which would make it either dishonest or dangerous for him to accept belief at that particular time. It is not enough to think that since Christianity is truth, then it does not matter how clumsily it is rammed into people. If it is truth, then it must be sought always upon the far side of others' integrity. We must trust the reality of faith enough to believe that if we encourage others in a fearless search for truth and do not worry where it leads them, it will in the end lead to Christ.

For many, of course, the search is not primarily an intellectual search, but a search for a healing of the personality and its wounds. The man who rejects God because he identifies him with the father who rejected him, the woman who is locked in neurotic anxiety or depression, is not principally concerned in discovering a faith but in finding healing for nagging emotional wounds. If we think that the answer for such people is to be pressed immediately into the Christian camp, we may do more harm than good. All that we may be able to do for other people is to care about their suffering and ease it if we can; to tell them the truth, to encourage them to live in the real world rather than in a fantasy one. But then this *is* a step towards Christ. We may only be able to offer Christ to the agnostic through our love and honesty, not through the doctrine, the sacraments, or the fellowship of the Church. But then to each the food he is able to digest.

If, however, the Christian challenge to the agnostic is to the greatest integrity of which he is capable, the greatest self-knowledge, the most valiant attempts to live in reality instead of in fantasy, then the Christian himself needs to change out of recognition. The Church has encouraged us to believe that all that is needed for spiritual health is the routine of prayer and the liturgy, of confession and the sacraments. These things are, of course, infinitely precious, a life-giving and sanity-preserving framework of life and more besides; the foretaste of the abundant living talked about in the gospels. If one spends much time among practicing Christians one does find people who have been strangely and marvellously liberated by them and by the loving which springs from them. Yet the disturbing fact remains that too many who faithfully practice these things do not seem liberated people, but people as narrow, or more narrow, than those who have never been exposed to the faith. One thinks of the kind of Christian who cannot for one moment tolerate having his beliefs questioned or challenged; the sort who turned so furiously upon the Bishop of Woolwich; the sort who cannot imagine that outside his own ethic there can be any good or beauty or love.

It may be true, as Jung and others have noticed, that religion is a specific against neurosis, but it is by no means an infallible specific, and it can breed neuroses of its own. Harry Williams in *Objections to Christian Belief* has described the damage feelings of guilt did to one Christian:

"One night he had a nightmare which proved to be

a turning point in his life. In his dream he was sitting in a theatre watching a play. He turned round and looked behind him. At the back of the theatre there was a monster in human form who was savagely hypnotizing the actors on the stage, reducing them to puppets. The spectacle of this harsh, inhuman puppeteer exercising his hypnotic powers so that the people on the stage were completely under his spell and the slaves of his will—this spectacle was so terrifying that the man awoke trembling and in a cold sweat. After several months he gradually realized that the monster of the nightmare was the god he was really worshipping. . . . And to this god he had painfully to die. He had to accept the terrible truth that the practice of his religion had been a desperate attempt to keep his eyes averted from the monster of the nightmare. He had thought that, with many failures, it is true, but according to his powers, he was responding to God's love. His dream showed him that he was a devil's slave—his devotion and his goodness being a compulsive response to a deeply embedded feeling of guilt, and this, in spite of his regular use of sacramental confession. . . . Life and behaviour based on feelings of guilt excludes charity. To be bullied, compelled, by subtle inner unidentifiable fear to apparent worship and goodness is to destroy the self. And without a self one cannot give."

This describes one kind of Christian who appears to be busy with learning to love but is in fact busy about something quite different—appeasing his own miserable sense of guilt. There are, however, so many ways of using faith to avoid seeing the truth about ourselves. There are the sort of Christians who believe Christianity is something to do with being a good citizen and have it all mixed up with ideas of patriotism. There are the sort of Christians who believe Christianity is a device for stopping venereal disease and illegitimate babies, and for shoring up family life against the inroads of divorce and lust.

In all these cases the faith which should have led to enlightenment and self-knowledge has become a means of evading reality, of retiring into a fantasy world which is safer and nicer than the real one. Within fantasies such as these, men do not have to grow, nor to grow up, do not have to pay the terrible price of maturity, which is to bear the knowledge of their fears and their desires.

An interesting question is why the Church has sometimes been reluctant to accept psychological insights which might help their members far more effectively than the superficial process of confession. It seems probable that it is because to admit the limitations imposed upon the personality by certain sorts of upbringing or childhood experience appears to diminish the degree of choice and responsibility which the Church has insisted men enjoyed. If you admit, say, that a child deprived of affection is predisposed to steal, then you seem to have damaged the doctrine of free-will.

How often in the moral field do we make a genuinely free choice? Quite apart from our unconscious fears and desires which influence our decisions in ways we cannot know, so much depends in any situation upon our personality and our upbringing, upon past situations and the degree to which in them we have conquered or failed. Yet there is a way and a time in which free-will operates. We always have the choice of listening or of not listening to other people when they tell us about ourselves. It can be exceedingly painful when other people—our friends, relatives, neighbours, colleagues—bring us face to face with our failures, the way in which we continually hurt, disappoint, or fail others, and it is always tempting to find one excuse or another for dismissing their remarks. Yet this is one of the areas where genuine choice operates and where growth can begin. It is much more fruitful than the kind of self-examination which the Church has often urged upon disciples, if only because our worst failings are usually those which never occur to us. A thoroughly perceptive remark about us from a friend nearly always comes as a surprise; in all our thoughts about ourselves we had never hit on that way of seeing ourselves, and yet we know at once, or in the course of time, that it is the truth. I am not myself clear how the confessor, who may know little of a penitent outside the confessional, can perform such a necessary service, a service which may only be possible for those closely or emotionally involved. I do not deny the sacramental quality of confession. I do feel, however, that it is sacramental much more widely than the usual conception of it suggests. That it is sacramental, for example, on occasions between husband and wife, between one friend and another, between parent and child, between psychiatrist and patient, at the moment when the emotional crisis is reached, the sting drawn from the old, tormenting wound, and peace becomes a possibility at last.

The Church has too often encapsulated confession, sedated its agony within a safe, pain-killing formula, and so concealed the fact that its real purpose (a purpose very similar to that of the analyst) is to uncover the wound so that it may heal.

If the Christians hope to hold a fruitful dialogue with the agnostics then they must show, by their peace and their maturity, that they have been to the confessional, the confessional of their own intimate relationships in which the truth about them stands revealed at last—and have borne their own particular crisis. This makes them worthy to be heard not as Christians—the agnostic may have small use for Christians—but as men brave enough to seek and face the truth, wherever it may lead them. The Christian's faith is that truth leads to Christ, is itself Christ. The agnostic has made no such discovery, but is as anxious as the Christian to solve the incidental problems of living truthfully, the problems of relationship. In their common effort towards courage, knowledge, and love, they find themselves thinking and speaking in each other's language.

The Christians too must love "this world" not in a desperate attempt to be "with it" but for its own sake. It is beautiful enough if we do not perpetually sour it with condemnation. If all that the God-dimension has done for us is to make us look down on "the world," like the kind of Englishman who despises England because he has discovered the Continent, or the American who is contemptuous of America because he has discovered Europe, then it were better for us not to have discovered God. The purpose of the Christian revelation was not that we should end up like Bertrand Russell, claiming that "life is horrible, horrible, horrible." The Christian has discovered meaning and joy on the far side of waste and agony; he has experienced the resurrection.

V

The Way Forward

So far I have been critical and negative about the Church's attitude to the world and to the unbeliever. It is time perhaps to be more positive, to suggest the way forward from failure and non-communication.

Peter Lennon's article in *The Guardian* already quoted offers a clue. He was delighted to find "no trace of a clerical attitude" in Father Kelly's approach to *L'Avventura*. What one longs to see is no trace of a clerical attitude towards life, but a joyful and imaginative opening towards people, towards experience, and towards art. This can only be achieved when fear is exorcised, when nothing and nobody seems a threat to our beliefs since we have encountered all our demons and discovered that they do not overcome us.

The opening must take place above all in the Christians' attitude towards his neighbour, towards everyone with whom he comes into contact. If he is deeply afraid of contact with other people, afraid of emotion, afraid of lowering his defences, afraid of the other sex, then his discipleship must begin with the humbling and painful attempt of curing this. For the vocation of the Christian is to love, and if he is isolated, cold, and invulnerable then he is useless for his purpose and had better be a tycoon or a statesman or a demagogue. For what men need from the Christian and from his priests is not uplift or moralizing or condemnation, but love. The kind of parson who can never stop his inconsequential chatter long enough to let anything important be said, the kind of Christian who cannot allow his relationships ever to become deep enough for others to trust him not to make judgments, both fail abysmally in love.

In the effort to learn more about loving, Christians need to mop up secular insights with shameless greed. It does not matter where the knowledge and understanding come from—whether from the Freudians, from the Jungians, from sociologists or social workers, from existentialists or "new moralists"—if it illuminates the dark and unredeemed areas of ourselves, if it makes the lonely, lost, and unloved aspect of other people easier to understand, then we must absorb it and use it. Brave and brilliantly intelligent attempts are being made in our time to reach the most hopeless and the most isolated—to penetrate the logic of schizophrenia, for example, to solve the riddle of the psychopath, the criminal, the sexually deviant. Here is the working of love.

Christians do not need humility, charity, and enthusiasm only in the field of psychology and sociology, but also in the arts, where with baffling stupidity they so often fail to see the wood for the trees. Like the fat white woman whom nobody loves they walk through the pastures of modern writing and modern thinking missing the courage and the honesty of its humanism, noticing only that God is not obviously praised. By these standards a poor novel written by a Christian is better than the pagan Lawrence's hymn to tenderness and sexual joy, a cheap plaster image of the Virgin Mary is better than one of Francis Bacon's tortured attempts to paint the crucifixion, a television program which puts across a naïve, uncontroversial version of the Christian faith is better than one where men try to utter the real inhibitions which hold them back from God.

The result is bitterly tragic. It is that Christians too often breed and encourage the second-rate, the timid and the shoddy, and expel from their midst those who are great with integrity, who are groaning and straining to give birth to the truth that is in them. It is not by accident that few great painters, or writers, or thinkers of our time are Christian. The Christians have treated them with the fear and hostility once shown to lepers, have lined up on the side of artistic reaction, of unoriginal thought, of the safe, the cosy and the cowardly. To speak to the intelligent and the discerning it will be necessary to discover contemporary art and literature and thought, and to rejoice in its quality and its courage.

For having failed in this, Christians have been beaten back to the role of social reformers, and even here they are less effective than many unbelieving men and women who have opened themselves, fearlessly and joyfully, to the spirit of the times. It is not hard

81

to understand why this should be. If we seal ourselves off from what is actually going on—and if we neglect, or believe ourselves superior to, the most articulate of our contemporaries this is what we are doing—then we can never minister effectively to the wounds of society. We shall be answering questions that no one is asking, repeating clichés that have become meaningless, while men cry out for the help we are too blind to give.

If we are to see clearly then we must look at the pictures, must read the books, must see the films and the plays and listen to the discussion. If we understand only a little of it it does not matter. What does matter is that the process of questioning, or arguing, of understanding, should continue ceaselessly within us, so that we become a true part of the dialogue of our time. We must stop being afraid of experience, of new ideas, even those which we cannot immediately fit into the framework of belief. It is sin for us to try to carve experience to fit religion, wrong for us to twist the problems to fit our answers, wicked of us to sit in judgment upon our own generation, ludicrous of us to try to bludgeon others (by guilt or fear) into our way of thinking.

A real change of heart among the Christians would mean that the superior, threatening note disappeared, and archi-episcopal and episcopal utterances plunged into the heart of the things which really trouble thinking men and women at the moment. There would be less about the symptomatic things, such as outspoken books, and much more about the roots of human lovelessness. There would be infinitely more concern, for example, about the rising homelessness and the impossible living conditions in which many families have to exist. There would be concern about the disgraceful, spirit-breaking conditions in our prisons where, in many cases, little or no attempt is made to redeem. There would be anxiety about the overcrowding in schools which exposes children, whose proper craving is to be noticed and valued, to the impersonal atmosphere which is the enemy of love.

The value, as I see it, of the speeches, statements, and sermons of primates and bishops, is not that they have much impact on the pagan world but that they can rally Christian opinion and action to a point in the lines of love where ignorance, prejudice, hatred, or evil can be seen to have broken through.

The Church could, if it chose, be much quicker on its feet than the Welfare State. It could be daring in pioneering new schemes to meet new human needs, provided it was ruthless enough to hand the schemes over to the State once it had been proved that they worked. For example, how much better it would be to surrender the expenses of church schools and church training colleges now that the State can do the job as well or better, and concentrate financial resources in an area of human experience where the need is much more acute.

In the field of mental illness, say, where the need for experiment, for new and varied methods, for daring thought, for money, is acute, the churches might make a gigantic contribution to the love they claim to believe in. I am reminded of one experimenter I know, a devout Christian herself, who made a home where people on the verge of breakdown or trying to find their feet after a spell in a mental hospital, could come and stay. She was extraordinarily successful in building a sense of community, and in helping people suffering from an acute sense of isolation to learn new and happier relationships. Here was a scheme which, since it had been seen to meet a pressing need, might have been adopted by the Church who could have taken all the financial problems involved upon its shoulders, and built up a scheme for similar houses in other parts of the country. Needless to say, this particular home still limps along on individual charity, turning away innumerable people desperate for help.

There is boundless scope for building communities in which people with neurotic troubles could learn how to make new and better relationships. We have a society which has attempted to abolish real poverty, but which in doing so has uncovered a new, and equally tragic set of problems, which affluence cannot heal. It is described in so many ways and by so many different kinds of people. Psychiatrists talk of people becoming "de-personalized"; the rest of us may talk of feeling lonely, cut off, isolated, unable when surrounded by other people to break through to them and achieve any real contact.

"Loneliness" is the word that brings the tears. An editor of a national newspaper has only to print an article dealing, however superficially, with this subject and the letters will begin to pour in by the hundreds.

The letters come from people in all age groups and of all classes. From the young or middle-aged living alone in bed-sitting rooms, from the old, from housewives and young mothers, from students and from men and women successfully established in a job or profession. Something precious is missing from our society which was there in the days of shared hardship, of rigid social structure and of war; a quality of cohesion. We cannot, even if we wished, go back to the days of poverty or of war to heal our wounds. If we are wise we do not pretend that a return to old-style religion is the answer. Carstairs aptly describes how far out contemporaries have come from that particular haven. "There are, of course, still some people who sincerely believe in the teaching of the Christian Church, but the Church's own statistics show that they have become a minority group—a rather small minority. The rituals of the Church persist . . . but one suspects that they are often mere forms, as empty of significance as the habit of touching wood for luck. Most people today lack religious conviction; in its place there persists a left-over jumble of ethical precepts, now bereft of their significance, and the widespread habit of occasional private prayer to a God in whom most people only half believe."

Yet Carstairs also describes the drab agony which the retreat of religion leaves behind it: "During this year over 5,000 people will have committed suicide in Britian: at a conservative estimate, another 30,000 will have attempted suicide, and many thousands more will have lived through—or are still contending with—a state of depression in which life becomes a pointless misery. Apart from those who are seriously depressed there are many more who lead a lack-lustre existence 'living and partly living'; and there are others whose dissatisfaction with life bursts out in acts of violence. A smouldering sense of defeat sometimes can break out in this way. Murder is not infrequently followed by the suicide of the murderer; but this association is found more often in the suicides of poor people than in those of the better-off. If there is this aggressive accompaniment of melancholia, may there not be an element of depression and despair behind the increasing number of violent crimes in our society. One of the inescapable, and still unexplained realities of life now is the recent recrudescence of violence which reversed the trend of the previous hundred years, and which has contributed to the almost threefold increase in prison population since 1938. Why is it that grown men and women, no less than teen-agers, are registering this unmistakable vote of no confidence in a society which has in so many ways improved their physical and material conditions of life?"

Among the Christians there are many with a facile answer to isolation, meaninglessness, depression, and violence. Their answer is a stiffening of the faithful. Refusing to believe that religion is faced with a new situation that needs a new solution, they claim that the answer is to force everyone back into the mould. Some refuse even to notice that the mould is broken, and believe that those of us who insist that it is are behaving hysterically. The Archdeacon of Bodmin writing in *Prism* in July 1964 puts the old argument persuasively:

"As I look back over my own life as a priest, what are the things to which I cling and on which I depend? They are, I hope, the Eucharist at the centre of it all, the daily office, regular meditation and intercession, confession, the annual retreat, and an attempt (and only a poor attempt) to live a life with some sort of discipline and scale of values, and all lit up by the round of fast and feast in the Christian year. . . . They are the mainstay of a way of life by which very many priests strive to live and order their lives, and for the reason that they are the means by which the old doctrines are experienced and made contemporary. Are these ways outmoded by the younger generation? God save us if they are."

God save us indeed, but in the meantime we long for men like the Archdeacon to try to see the force of our argument. Of course, the life he outlines may lead to holiness and may make the old doctrines contemporary. What bothers me is how often it fails to do anything of the kind. It is perfectly possible for men to lead the life he outlines down to its last detail and remain blind and unloving. The very confidence such piety gives sets a divine authority upon intolerance and prejudice. The men who burned the heretics, who failed to protest at Hitler's massacre of the Jews, were faithful in church-going and constant in prayer. Nevertheless I do believe the Archdeacon's program may be life-giving for those who can do it, provided it is accompanied by an openness to other ways of living and a readiness to admit that none of us has a short-cut to insight.

But the final failure of the Archdeacon's way of life may lie in the fact that many simply could not carry it out. There are many Christians who go to church for lack of any better way to show loyalty to their beliefs, and many more who stay away, but who find the services, the simple teaching about prayer and meditation, the formula of confession, almost meaningless, or worse, a threat to their integrity.

For these things may demand so many private reservations, such as a determined attempt to ignore much of what one knows of one's own psychology and that of other people. Within the formula of confession, one can admit the same sin over and over again knowing even while one confesses that the power is simply not within one to refrain from doing the same thing again when the same situation occurs. Is it really one's own most grievous fault? In my own case, I know that sometimes it is and sometimes it isn't. That I have some free-will in some situations, but not in all.

So is the way to restore cohesion to our society to dragoon people back into the churches? Even if this were the answer we could not apply it, but in any case it would not do. It is too late to tempt people back into childlike dependence. It would be wicked of the church to try to shrink them in this way, through good and brave to try to stretch them to make a discovery on the far side of their integrity. And this can only lie in the direction of urging men and women to seek the

God who does not live only in the churches but in marriage, friendship, neighbourliness, and work.

So that while there may still be a place for the kind of religious life outlined by the Archdeacon, those who live it should recognize that for many other Christians the vocation is to live enclosed by and in the secular world, loving it and knowing it with the same dedication that the monk offers to his community.

This kind of Christian finds himself at loggerheads at every turn with the sort of Christian who feels that the answer to illegitimate babies, venereal disease, and perversion, is stricter morals, stiffer laws, censorship of books and plays, and more church-going. The secular Christian objects that these remedies are not practical, since goodness cannot be imposed but must spring spontaneously out of a way of life. And that the way of life in turn must not be imposed but must spring out of men's beliefs and their search for truth.

Compared to the moralistic Christian, the secular Christian appears a vague fellow, busying himself with picking up the pieces and putting balm on the effects, claiming that he cannot control the cause. All that he can do is to seek truth and love both within the Church and outside it, and by his seeking help to make the climate of society more loving so that it will not seek substitutes instead of true relationships, will discover that sexual intercourse without love is meaningless, and that pornography is boring and unsatisfying. It is a long way round, but, even in terms of pregnant schoolgirls or the spread of venereal disease, the shortest way home.

But there is another more terrible sense in which the secular Christian dissociates himself from the worry of the moralistic Christian, and it is one of the things which help to make Christianity the scandal that it is. There is a point at which he feels it doesn't matter, that life is not about morals but about love, and that for even the most loveless of deeds there is redemption. This puts him in danger of underestimating suffering, but if he does not so do, if he remains faithful to others during their crucifixions and faithful to God during his own, then he rediscovers the resurrection.

Many of the worst problems which face us call not so much for tension and conscious effort to solve them as relaxation and calmness. Racialism, for example, which has caused such desperate suffering in our time and which has by no means finished with us yet, will be healed eventually not simply by the brave and strenuous efforts of the Civil Rights workers in America, or by the courageous stand by the dwindling opposition in South Africa, but by the quiet self-knowledge which comes from understanding our own motives.* Violence, crime, despair, might yield to new insights about relationships—the relationship of the child within the family, the individual within society. War, which has scourged mankind throughout history, might be stamped out if we cared to learn more about the function of aggression. Until a few years ago, it seemed unbelievable that tuberculosis or typhoid or diphtheria could be controlled, but the upsurge of

---

* See The Back Together Heart, by Sarah Patton Boyle. A Forward Movement Miniature Book. 25 cents.

confidence and belief in medical advance made such a victory possible.

What is needed now, and who better to carry it out than the Christian Church which has preached the remedy throughout its history, though it has not always practiced it, is a new understanding of love. As there is a hygiene of the body which, properly carried out, strengthens its resistance to disease, so there is a hygiene of the mind and of the spirit. We know more and more about the emotional environment that a child needs to grow up fearless and outgoing, able to give love and receive it. To my surprise the Church talks little about these requirements, but far too much and far too critically about the adolescents and adults whose lives have already been irreparably damaged by emotional impoverishment.

Talking of the qualities which our society desperately needs to cultivate and which so far it has succeeded in creating in only a small minority—intellectual curiosity, tolerance and consideration for others, spontaneous emotionl responsiveness to people and to ideas, aesthetic taste and creativity—Carstairs attributes our failure to the following causes:

"Children grow up with personalities crippled by the economics of scarcity: scarcity above all of affection and emotional security, which renders them liable, in later life, to personal isolation, suspicion, and despair. It may be instructive to compare this situation with that of thirty, or fifty, or a hundred years ago, when a much higher proportion of children grew up in homes which were not only emotionally but also materially impoverished. We have made progress in reducing the amount of severe poverty in our society: our next task is to try to ensure that children are not deprived of the emotional sustenance which they need in order to develop into well-balanced beings."

This, however, is a task which will take several generations. In the meantime we all have to recognize our own emotional inadequacies and the way these interact upon our children and our friends. Failure to do so means that we are seriously handicapped in offering the love which we claim to be the Christian contribution to society.

Some of the loneliest people in our community are those who have failed in one way or another in the ideal code of behaviour we have laid down; the unmarried mother, the young man who has discovered that he is homosexual, the divorcee, the man or woman who is haunted by thoughts of suicide and may have made more than one attempt at it, the middle-aged man who has committed adultery. Would any of these people turn automatically to the local Christian community, in the confident expectation that they would receive love and understanding?

Some of these people might, and do, turn to a parish priest for comfort and help, or to some other Christian organization. But if the priest is to solve their loneliness permanently, and is to offer something more valuable than a clinging and dependent relationship upon himself, then he needs an accepting community into which he can introduce those who suffer acutely from a sense of exclusion.

A few churches have such a nucleus of people, but the majority of church-folk are not like that, partly because of an ignorance and a lack of imagination which over-simplifies moral behaviour, partly because they fear that to forgive anti-social attitudes is to condone them. This is the old fear, already mentioned in earlier chapters, that truth will not prevail, that the moral structure of a nation is so fragile that it needs elaborate defences. Christians, it seems to me, have to choose between the safety of "morals" and the danger of love. It is my own belief that Christ's teaching was principally about the latter, but that if you do reach men and women to love God and love their neighbour then morals take care of themselves.

The literal loving of the neighbour is something preachers might mention much more often than they do. We are good at getting ourselves so immersed in the sea of religious metaphor that the obvious disappears. In our figurative vagueness we can manage to lose sight of the fact that we are supposed to love the people who live next door and that we have to solve our problems of relationsip within our own marriages and with our own children. Love must be a process of learning to be vulnerable—to one another, to ideas, to knowledge, to the arts, even to the injuries which the forces of evil constantly try to inflict. It is impossible to love without getting hurt, if only because the loveless may be incapable of responding to love. This is what is meant about taking up the cross and following Christ. Being a Christian means believing that love overcomes lovelessness, though at a cost.

Though Christians ought to be giving themselves to such obvious duties as setting up housing trusts, or agitating politically for more action on housing; though they should be showing up racialism by forming firm friendships which ignore racial barriers; though they should be exerting themselves in their own neighbourhoods by removing overcrowding in schools or miserable living conditions for the old; although they should do all these things, none of it will be any good except as an exercise in humanism unless it is accomplished by a ploughing of the heart and mind and imagination which will make it possible for the seed of love to grow.

What troubles most of us in our loving is a desperate fear of failure. Canon Rhymes recently quoted a tragic remark by T. E. Lawrence which described the malaise in an acute form:

"There was my striving to be liked so strong and nervous that I could never open myself friendly to another. The terror of failure in an effort so important made me shrink from trying."

There must be innumerable people who could now echo these words. The roots of such fears which choke love like weeds need repeated examination. Partly they spring from failures in loving within the family and within society; partly, also, from a horror of the body and its desires which the Church has done much to encourage Lawrence himself could not bear to be touched.

Yet to be comforted, to be assured that we are valuable and important, we need to be touched. We need our hands to be shaken, our cheeks to be kissed, our shoulders to be embraced, with the quick sympathy and affection of friendship or of kinship.

With the sophistication of post-Freudians we know that there is a sexual element in all our friendships and all our family loves. So much the better. It helps us to rid our sexual nature of the accretions of guilt and obscenity which centuries of puritanism have heaped upon it.

There is so much in our society which separates and isolates men, and the Church should express its penitence for teaching which has added to the burden. The danger nowadays is that people cannot find any valid way of coming close to others.

VI

In the Midst of the World

To write as I have written inevitably suggests an arrogance and a self-assurance which is hard for others to forgive. Also, in one who claims to be a Christian and an Anglican, it indicates disloyalty. We are fond of talking of the Church as our mother, and our fellow-Christians as our brothers and sisters, so that any public criticism is interpreted in Christian circles as a washing of dirty linen in public which is unkind and unnecessary. Indeed the anger against Dr. Robinson, Dr. Vidler, Mr. Harry Williams and others was directed at them because they had discussed publicly subjects which Christians had discussed privately for years. Why then do I indulge in this perverse activity? Partly, undoubtedly, because I am shocked and frightened at the Church's growing preoccupation with its public image at the expense of its private integrity. Recently I attended a press party given by a bishop whose work I have long admired. The conversation there, which to both the bishop and the journalists concerned seemed perfectly normal, was about how to get a good image of the Church in the press. At first sight perhaps an admirable idea. Much nicer and more comfortable for the Church, much more likely to get people turning up at her services, if the papers are full of punchy quotations from sermons or accounts of Christian good works than if they lift some Vicar's bilious remarks about the younger generation.

Yet the Church stands to witness to the truth, even when the truth brings it no personal advantage. Where is the recognition—a recognition desperately needed in contemporary life—that "good publicity" represents as wrong a distortion of the truth as the other kind?

Is it really allowed to Christians to be so concerned about the effect they are having? Is not this a case where our left hand should not know or care what our right hand is doing? The only publicity Christians are allowed is the kind that comes from love and goodness being practiced out of deep conviction. If publicity is to become a touchstone of Christian judgment, then the Christian gospel is subtly altered. According to the gospel, for example, the defaulting Vicar who made such poor publicity for his cause, might in the humility and poverty of his weakness become a more potent instrument of God's glory than a man who had never been broken. The fruits of the spirit—the hallmarks of a man who has committed himself to being a Christian—are love, joy, peace, longsuffering, gentleness, goodness, faith, meekness, temperance. It follows from this—to anyone who knows the world of publicity—that Christians who live in obedience are almost never going to make the headlines, become television personalities, or have a good public image, because to do these things it is necessary to permit a tampering with the truth of one's own personality. Christians are, or should be, anti-image men, smashing this particular golden calf as contemptuously as Moses smashed the other, laughing to scorn the idea that they should bow down to it. Life, or at any rate the new life, makes it absurd that we should serve such a limited idol as the public image.

What if we don't bow down but busy ourselves instead with the proper preoccupation of Christians— the love of God and the love of our neighbour. Much of the time we shall be ridiculed, or (much more painfully) ignored as being outside the circle of people who matter, and outside the arena where the important work goes on. But whether we are truly out of the arena depends upon ourselves, upon whether we are equipped with the knowledge, the insight and the love to say anything relevant to the condition of the world. It is part of our conviction that truth makes itself heard. That the words of a Bonhoeffer, smuggled out of a Nazi prison, hacked out of his own conflict and agony, can reach and change a whole generation of Christians. That the words of a Father Huddleston or an Archbishop Joost de Blank, obstinately proclaiming love and equality in Christ, can reach the conscience of the world without the help, initially, of a vast publicity machine. The Church, of all institutions, must believe in the simplicity of love and truth and their ability to make their way against all obstacles, even against the obstacles of death and destruction. This *is* our gospel, a gospel which we betray if the Church gets herself up to tempt Fleet Street and the world of television. For those who sell themselves all have one drawback in common. They no longer have anything real to give, only a pale and piteous imitation of love and of genuine relationship.

My bitterness does not stop there, however, but is entangled at every point where I have tried to understand what being a Christian means nearly two thousand years after the Word was first made flesh. You may say that I have projected upon the Church and upon the Christian situation my own failure, my own problems of relationship, my own humiliating sense of frustration. But then I am a member of the Christian body, and my problem is that of the other members even if none of them had felt it themselves. There is evidence, however, that very many of the others share it; what makes our rage and bewilderment especially hard to bear is the knowledge that very many religious leaders do not even choose to see that there is any problem at all.

I spoke earlier of the house for mentally ill people run by a convinced and practicing Christian. She told me of one of her patients, a man suffering from paranoic fears that God was persecuting him, who went finally and dreadfully mad one night during a thunderstorm. He stood naked upon the stairs, screaming with a terrible intensity, "a great roar of grief" she called it "showing what it meant to be a man in pain."

Now I am not (I hope) going mad, and I am only intermittently in pain, but I share that man's longing to pierce the stifling and claustrophobic world with a stab of urgency and reality. Except that, unlike him, I am not quarrelling with the Universe but with the Church which claims that it is not narrow, not suffocating, not a coffin for the spirit.

It is a great arrogance to describe one's conversion, but what happened to me was this. In a situation in which I felt a crippling sense of guilt, a sense of total meaninglessness, a sense of growing isolation from those around me, I suffered, to my surprise, a revelation of God. I had never had much sense of God previously. Like most children brought up in this country I had gone occasionally to church, had endured school prayers, never guessing that the ritual incantations about penitence, forgiveness, and love had any more meaning than the jingoistic incantations about patriotism and sacrifice which get cut down to size in the realities of war.

But God was suddenly someone experienced, asserting with tenderness, the beauty and strength of which nearly annihilated me altogether, that I was loved and I was forgiven. It is almost impossible to explain to a non-Christian what this experience consists of, nor why it changes every relationship and every attitude. Abelard came nearest to expressing the heat and the passion of it.

"Set on fire as we are by so great a benefit from the Divine grace, true charity should fear nothing at all. . . . And so our redemption is that supreme love manifested in our case by the passion of Christ, which not only delivers us from the bondage of sin, but also acquires for us the liberty of the sons of God; so that we may fulfil all things from the love rather than from the fear of him, who, as he himself bears witness, showed us grace so great that no greater can be found."

Peter Abelard lived the sort of life which would have brought the Church bad publicity in the Sunday newspapers, and in the wave of puritanism now blowing across the churches it may be too much to expect anyone to appreciate his note of authority. No doubt he would have to endure the blanket condemnation at present thrown over the whole school of "new moralists."

But "set on fire"? Fulfilling "all things from the love rather than from the fear" of God? Where nowadays in the Church do we find that triumphant recognition that the love of God is the grandest of grand passions, or that resolute rejection of guilt is the spur?

But to go back to the process of conversion. As Charles Williams explains in *The Descent of the Dove* the problem for the Christian is time. How is he to make sense of his singular experience in terms of time? What does he do about it, day in and day out?

For those who undergo the shattering experience of conversion there is another problem which often precedes this, which is how to endure the shock of what has happened. In *Beyond all Reason* Morag Coate describes how, unable to find anyone to share her sudden knowledge of God, she drove herself on to ever more esoteric spiritual adventures until she fell over the cliff of schizophrenia. Few people who have undergone a conversion experience will find this hard to understand. Romantic love, if it goes wrong, brings the most stable people near to psychosis. Religious passion uncovers the great agonies of acceptance and rejection at a still deeper level, healing or wounding the personality at its center. In a foreword to Miss Coate's book, the psychiatrist R. D. Laing suggests that one of the author's greatest misfortunes was that, at the time when she most needed to share her shattering experience of God, she did not "find her guru." I was luckier in that I knew a priest who had both acted as a kind of catalyst of truth in my first critical examination of religion before my conversion, and who was able to bear the first shock of it with me afterwards. I owe him an immense debt, and I hope he will not interpret anything I have written as an attack upon him or upon his explanation of Christian doctrines and ideas which at the time meant so much to me.

But the Church has to exist in time; I had to be a Christian in time, and the disillusion cut deep. Not the disillusion of finding that the certainty of conversion did not last. After fourteen years the awareness of love and forgiveness remains as strong as if it had happened an hour ago. Not the disillusion of discovering how hard it is to love, or how terrifying evil can be if you challenge it directly.

The disillusion I am talking about is the disillusion

of discovering that the Church can behave like anti-Christ, that Christians can use their faith as a protection against ever seeing the truth or against exposing themselves to life and experience in any genuine way at all.

Certain exclusive sects demonstrate this neurotic use of faith in its most extreme form. By the rigidity of their rules they postulate a certainty which, in the nature of things, none of us can have, which excuses them from the pangs of intellectual conflict. Then, with a typically neurotic withdrawal from difficult or challenging relationships, they restrict their friendships to those with the sect.

The larger denominations to some extent overcome these dangers, simply by the variety of their members, and the quality of the minds they are able to attract and hold. Yet do not all the recent religious controversies indicate a similar fear of facing new ideas, a similar terror that spiritual and intellectual security is about to be threatened? It is this which prevents the easy, spontaneous dialogue which might make belief seem vivid and possible to our contemporaries, which might create the climate of thinking and talking in which people of all kinds and backgrounds might become aware of God.

In *Come out the Wilderness* Bruce Kenrick described an evening among the toughs of East Harlem when for a little while Christianity came spontaneously alive. "One evening an expert musician with special knowledge of jazz was the guest. During the singing time before the service he sat at the piano, trying out different rhythms. He asked, 'What is the text for tonight?' 'Seek, and ye shall find,' came the answer, 'Ask, and it shall be given you; knock, and it shall be opened unto you.' He began to line out a beat, humming, 'Seek, seek, seek.' Some of the boys who usually stood outside or in the back during this time came up and gathered round the piano and began to join in. Before the service started one hundred young people seated in the sanctuary of the church had worked out a swing version of the text. Those who had been hardest to reach in the past and most bored by many of the Sunday nights were the most eager participants. As the worship leader wrote later, 'When the time came for the reading of the Scripture, somehow these verses did not come out to the same ears that had heard them before. In a new way there was a listening, as if to say, "These are my words; I know them; they are part of me." ' "

I am not pretending that jazzing up the mass is necessarily the answer for most of us. What I do profoundly believe is that truth has a million ways of expressing itself as yet untried and that Christians should turn with delight to all of them, bravely confident that Christ is to be found in the new as in the old.

For the nostalgic preoccupation with the old—old architecture, old forms of liturgy, ancient vestments, and the failure of Christians to find dynamic new forms of expression—indicates that the faith is being used as an escape from contemporary life which in itself borders upon the neurotic. This is religion used as a bolt-hole, not as a device for accepting reality. In a recent Jewish controversy a correspondent in the *Jewish Chronicle* expressed this as well as I have heard it expressed; his words might have been penned by ten thousand Christians up and down the land.

"As one of those who pops into synagogue occasionally to 'show his face' and who takes full advantage of what you term the undogmatic and flexible tradition of the United Synagogue, and who was in the same war as Dr. Brodie, I read the letters from enlightened doctors, professors and lecturers which you print with considerable amusement every week. But when it comes to the crunch you will find that the power lies, not with your clever doctors, professors, and lecturers, but with us unreasoning, illogical, paradoxical fellows who pay our money and take our choice.

"The Chief Rabbi and his ministers are there to be rigid on our behalf until we find time to do it ourselves, so you may be sure that our choice will not be the *Jewish Chronicle* or Rabbi Jacobs."

"Until we find time to do it ourselves" is the revealing phrase. This sort of faith is not the kind one goes to bed with and gets up with, eats and drinks, works and plays, laughs and cries, makes friends and makes love with. If it were truly those things we would become impatient with its archaisms, its incomprehensible language, its dry rot, and its hushed atmosphere. Instead it is a tiny peaceful garden into which one creeps when the pain of living gets too much, and the

Chief Rabbi, the Pope, the Archbishop of Canterbury are the head gardeners, obligingly keeping down the weeds and trimming the hedges.

All very nice for those who want that sort of thing, but most men are strong enough and wise enough to know that this will not do, and that if this is what the Church is offering then it is more honest to spurn it. Significantly when the Church tries to build and create something new, when it has the courage of its own convictions as it did at Coventry, then the unchurched world comes flocking to see. A word has been spoken in the vernacular, and at once people listen.

My disillusion was also a moral disillusion, however. I had thought that being a Christian meant trying, however clumsily, to recognize a relationship with God and with one's neighbour. But I heard innumerable clerics talking as if one must seek goodness not because it is reality, but because it preserves the fabric of our national life, maintains family life, prevents us going the nasty way of the Roman Empire. Why should we use God as a tool to keep Britain great? Just as if Britain were more than a grasshopper before that Majesty and that glory. How dare we employ him as a marriage guidance worker-cum-probation officer? If we do not love him, then neither our nation nor our family life matters very much. Except the Lord build the family, they labour in vain that build it; except the Lord keep the nation, the Watch Committee stirreth but in vain.

Disillusion spreads as one notices the lack of all real

tenderness in Christian pronouncements on those who have failed to maintain their moral standards, who have somehow or other lost their way in their attempt to find love. One of our Primates referred to boys and girls who are not virgins when they marry as "second-hand goods." The word "goods" implies that they are less than fully human, the word "second-hand" that they are slightly soiled, shabby, less precious than the others. Yet they are infinitely precious. Christ loved them so much that his heart and his body were broken for them. They were good enough for God to love, though not good enough for an archbishop.

We shall never be permitted to love our contemporaries, never heal the sores with which our society burns and aches, until Christians know how to put themselves imaginatively inside every wrong or anti-social act, and perceive in its hostility a stifled cry for love. So many necessary reforms in our society wait upon a Christian change of heart. Christians have often in the past led the way to new understanding and new compassion for those whom society as a whole did not want to comprehend. There is need now for this kind of imaginative involvement in mental illness, in the life of the young, in homosexual difficulties, in the isolation of old age, in criminal behaviour.

I did not finish the story of the young man who went mad. The director of the house where he was staying said, "When he began to scream I jumped out of bed and ran to him as quickly as I could. I knew that he needed to be comforted like a child and so I put my arm round his shoulders and told him that it was all right. But at the same time I was terrified that people who lived round about would complain about us and so damage our work. So I put one hand over his mouth to stifle the screams. (This house is set in a comfortable suburb where there are a number of well-supported churches.) And then I thought, but this *is* what is wrong. If people understand so little about mental illness, if they cannot see that there are times when a man has to open his mouth and roar with the agony of being human, then all our work is a waste of time. We cannot heal people unless the world outside can change."

Does Christian teaching make it easier or harder for such healing changes to occur? In theory, since it takes it for granted that we are all caught in the pain of sin (i.e. unreality) and we all spend much of our time trying to escape into unreality, then it makes little distinction in worth between one and another.

But in practice something quite different often happens, and the pharisaism which flows through our public life washes over into Christian judgments and relationships. To the pharisee a man who cannot conform to moral standards in his heart must at least appear to conform to them for the sake of some abstraction like "decency" or "the moral life of the nation."

If our morals are so rigid that they make it too difficult for men and women, for friends, for fellow-Christians, to admit to one another the wounds and the disabilities, the sins and the sense of isolation which trouble them, then it is the worse for morals. If we are going to use morals as a device for exclusion instead of inclusion, for refusing love instead of giving it, then it were better to cut them off and cast them from us.

The pharisee has made the mistake of shifting the emphasis from love to morals. It is for the Christian to shift the emphasis back again, noting as he does so that while good morals spring naturally out of love, love does not necessarily spring out of good morals. Good morals, if they force men into concealment and fear, are an instrument of the devil.

If we cannot live by love and forgiveness then the Christian is mistaken in thinking that the life of a Christ was a revelation of God, and individuals like myself are mistaken in supposing that when they received a personal revelation of love and forgiveness they were experiencing God.

But I am not disillusioned to the point of believing that I was deluded, nor that the Church's central teaching has been wrong all these years. I believe, on the contrary, that on that afternoon fourteen years ago, I saw reality more clearly than I had seen it before or since. I believe that the Church at its best has called men back time and again from the unrealities of power, of hate, of lies, of cruelty, of fame, of wealth, and reminded them that love is the way, the truth, and the life.

How can it achieve this once more? These chapters have been devoted to suggesting that the Church needs a new understanding of the world and of its needs. The most urgent of her priorities should be a turning outwards, away from the petty quarrels and worries which trouble her parishes and her assemblies, to look upon the world with joy and hope, pity and love. "So God loved the world," the priest reads off in the Communion service, "that he gave his only-begotten Son. . . ." *God* loved the world, but Christians seem unable to offer it anything but criticism and contempt.

If the Christians are truly confident in their God and in their faith, then they are free to launch new and more dangerous explorations into the human spirit. Medieval man put God at the limit of his mental world and chose to find him at the terrifying point where the land dropped away into nothingness. We are not that brave and intelligent. We have not yet dared to reach out for God at the expanded frontiers of thought, at the frontiers of physics, say, or psychology, or philosophy, or at the height of creative talent. So scared are we that if we broke through the moulds of religious thinking in a new bid for life, God would disappoint us, for we have chosen instead a wizened little deity who is ours to manipulate. Like some sad parson in *Lift Up Your Hearts* who has been told to give telling illustrations from everyday life, we are making our Lord and our God as petty and boring as we are ourselves.

The honest path for us now is to admit that we are not the know-alls we have long pretended, and that for the tiny fragment of God which we have seen and which has made us indelible Christians—there is infinitely more that we have not seen and have not begun to guess at. We are like archaeologists pedantically reconstructing a civilization from one piece of pottery while a whole city lies buried beneath our feet.

But we not only need daring, but also naturalness and honesty. We have for so long adopted a special tone of voice for talking about God, a quaint style for religious buildings, religious writing, religious talking, even religious printing. (I remember one friend of mine who wanted to start a new religious publication and could not woo the printer away from gothic conceits.) And we have fallen time and time again into the disastrous habit of talking in ideals, so that Christians collected together do not talk of what they actually are thinking and feeling, but of what they *ought* to be thinking and feeling.

There is a great need for us to recognize that in worshipping God we are frequently ridiculous, and that it will not do for us to conceal this knowledge from ourselves with a show of pomposity and an air of false reverence. The incongruity between man and God, the sheer difference of scale, is probably the fundamental joke, the father and mother, the Alpha and Omega, of all the jokes in the world. It's a pity people don't laugh at it more often.

It seems to me that the pomposity of Western religion, its tendency to fear the emotions and the realities of personal life, and try to take refuge in administrative achievement, may have to do with its determined masculinity. I remember being told in my early days as a Christian that what I felt didn't matter, that what *did* matter was the will; a piece of nonsense which any woman could recognize immediately as nonsense. It is not by chance that the position of women in our churches is such an ambivalent one; comparatively few women care to assert themselves outside the purely practical sphere, because the Church so rarely seems to be arguing in their language or about issues which seem to them important. Church discussion tends to begin with abstractions and work down eventually, if it gets so far, to the individuals involved in the situation. A true femininity begins with personalities and works outwards to abstractions. It is the Church's loss that she has so long despised feminine insights which might have taken her instinctively and quickly to situations which she has reached only slowly and by elaborate reasoning.

But the most profound reason for the Church's coldness and lack of connection is fear, a fear which expresses itself in the rigidity of worship, the timidity of sermons, the banality of public statements as much as in the pious horror directed against the "new moralists" and the Bishop of Woolwich. There is fear that the Christian sands are running out, that not only Christian morals but Christian beliefs and practices are in imminent danger of being swept away on the tide of secularism. I believe that, though this may not happen, we must learn to face with equanimity, even with enthusiasm, the prospect that it might happen, working out for ourselves in the process the kind of faith which could survive and make sense to us even in the most hostile conditions.

It was no accident that it was Bonhoeffer who explored the relevance of Christianity to a godless society. Deprived of his freedom and the right to work as a pastor, separated from friends and fellow-believers, confronted daily by brutality and himself the victim of it, it was not surprising that for him the old answers, even the old questions, made no sense. For the Christian in such circumstances the questions become very simple. What did Christ's death on the cross mean? Did he really triumph over evil or did evil triumph over him? Was there, *is* there a resurrection? Is it true that if we commit ourselves to love that the gates of hell shall not prevail against us? Or is the life of man a futile, meaningless, painful struggle in which the ruthless and the violent win every time?

The pain of the Christian vocation can be such that we do not often feel like asking these questions, and would much rather retreat into administration, respect-ability, good works, elaborate piety, or stern morality. But our contemporaries quite properly expect answers and are contemptuous of our attempts at escape. If *we* have lost our revelation about love and meaning, then we are of no use to the world at all. But if we can rediscover it, then we are at one with Christ, at one with the Suffering Servant, in building up the old wastes, raising up the former desolations, repairing the waste cities, the desolations of many generations. Like the Suffering Servant we shall be permitted to bind up the broken-hearted, to proclaim liberty to the captives and the opening of the prison to them that are bound, to proclaim the acceptable year of the Lord.

"And the Gentiles shall see thy righteousness, and all kings thy glory."

VII

Long Live the Church

WRITING as a Christian in the twentieth century, one cannot help sounding a little like the member of a beleaguered garrison, not so much, in the West at least, because one faces positive aggression, but because there is now a self-consciousness about being a Christian. So that there is either a slightly desperate note in one's voice, as one insists that the present age is no different from any other, or else one is struggling, often in darkness, with painful arguments about God, and the function of the Christian.

Philosophers talk of internal and external questions. Internal questions are those which you discuss within an established framework and discipline of thought. External questions are those which concern the actual framework itself. Where theology is concerned, nothing is easier, as we know, than to debate fascinating internal questions till the cows come home, if our fancy takes us that way. But for all but the most reactionary among us, there is now a suspicion that this is a neurotic defence against danger. We know very well that the time has come to face the external questions, the questions about the framework itself, about whether theology, as we have understood it, has a basis at all.

Harold Ross, the late editor of the "New Yorker," used to madden his staff by writing the words "Who He?" in the margins of their proofs, whenever they mentioned a celebrity. I suppose "Who He?" is the question we are now asking about God.

The Church had made certain affirmations about God, and our relationship to him, which seem to have a kind of practical efficacy where they are taken seriously, though it is a question why Christians have so often failed to take them seriously. But I believe the Church is right in saying that Man functions best when he sees himself as a creature, and is ready to admit that he derives life from God, and, apart from God, has no life. Without this admission, he is liable to be a devil incarnate, or to be smug, or to feel an aching hole at the center of his being. It seems also, on the same practical level, that we need to be able to admit that we are twisted, damaged, in a sense that we only understand imperfectly, but which hurts ourselves and others. We need a technique which will allow us to admit this, and which will restore to us the sense of fellowship we lose by it.

In addition, we need to strike some sort of bargain with our appetites, to achieve a balance between our passing needs and wishes, and the profounder needs, both of ourselves and others. One of the most persistent puzzles in all our lives, and it becomes more, not less, of a puzzle, if one is a Christian, is how far desire, of whatever kind, should be wrenched from an immediate object to serve a more remote good. Christians would recommend this more often than would most of their contemporaries. Malcolm Muggeridge, summing up Christ's teaching with admiration, epitomised it as "Want less." Muggeridge seems to be right in a way, but as we try to want less, we quickly discover that this does not kill our appetites; if things go well, we simply transfer our wanting to something bigger and better. And part of the value of the Church's affirmation has been that it has given us something bigger to want.

Then again the Church has affirmed our belonging to one another, and the responsibility this places upon each of us. It has denied us the right to make ourselves invulnerable behind our own cosy little ego boundary. It has forbidden us to perform the kind of lobotomy of the Spirit which will make us indifferent to others' distress. It has told us to notice, to listen, to suffer, and to learn.

And it has, of course, affirmed us not only as creature or sinner, as a bundle of restless appetites or as a neighbor, but as a person, a unique entity upon whom God has set his love and even his longing.

It has been able to do this so wholeheartedly because its major affirmation has been in God himself, repeatedly experienced as loving and forgiving, entering history as the perfectly faithful lover of mankind.

I crowned her with bliss and she me with thorn:
I led her to chamber and she me to die;
I brought her to worship and she me to scorn;

119

I did her reverence and she me villany. . . .
Her hate made never my love her foe. . . .

What shall I do now with my spouse
But abide her of my gentleness,
Till that she look out of her house
Of fleshly affection? Love mine she is;
Her bed is made, her bolster is bliss,
Her chamber is chosen; is there none mo?
Look out on me at the window of kindness,
Quia amore langueo.

The marvellous lack of inhibition with which such
mediaeval writers talked of God seems very alien to
our own period, but it is that kind of view, which, like
all great loves, transformed the whole landscape for
the believer.

But we are children of our age, and can, and must,
admit the doubts which blow across our minds like
clouds.

First, I suppose, is the huge unlikeliness of all the
traditional ideas about God and the Church when
seen against the backdrop of the twentieth century.
There are days, or anyhow moments, when to us God
just isn't, though to the traditionalist this is probably a
blasphemous statement.

Then there is the occasional feeling that God is
exactly what a man would construct to counter his
fears of living, just as a monkey, deprived of a mother,
will make a substitute mother figure out of a blanket.

And there must be, for us, anxieties about the divinity

of Jesus. A few years ago Christian writers used to say that, assuming his historical existence, Jesus was either a charlatan, a madman, or the son of God, and since he did not seem like the first two then he must be the last. Now, this seems psychologically naive. It may be that we no longer see a harsh division between the mad and the sane, or even the charlatans and the others, but we do know that it is possible for a man to become the expression of the unconscious longings and aspirations of a community, without himself fully comprehending what is going on. On a trivial level (if it *is* a trivial level), this is how film stars are born. It is what makes the Beatles a household word in Britain. On a more serious level, it is what sweeps a John F. Kennedy first to power, then to a kind of mythical death, or what allowed Germany to press power into the hands of a monster like Hitler.

It seems to me psychologically possible for Jesus to have been the expression of the unconscious longings of a deeply religious people, confined in an exclusive, compulsive, and narrowly legalistic form of religion. And if this was the case, then it seems likely they would need to kill him, as a man in Dallas, Texas, needed to kill Kennedy. Certain tensions are unbearable. They have to be broken before life can move on towards new understanding.

Then there is the problem of suffering. Much has been written trying to make Christian sense of the problem of pain, and I am not qualified to add to it, but what seems to be a matter of experience is that in the extremes of pain, either physical or mental, God is not. I don't mean that Christ did not enter into human pain, that pain does not have a fruitful outcome, or that those who suffer do not believe in God. I mean that what makes physical agony intolerable, or what tips mental suffering into momentary despair, is that for a particular person, at a particular moment, God is not, or at least does not appear to be, present, in any form in which the sufferer is capable of recognizing him.

The psychotherapist James Hillman, in his book "Suicide and the Soul" suggests that suicide is often an attempt to draw God from his covert, to persuade *deus absconditus* to reveal himself as the loving, gracious God.

Of the other strands which go to make up the tension of the faithful Christian, a number are concerned with the feeling that it is really quite easy to transcribe large chunks of Christian dogma and doctrine into psychological language. This does not necessarily make any of it untrue. If something is true, it is presumably true on many different levels, in different kinds of language, within different disciplines. But nevertheless there is a curious kind of pang as we note that none of our religious apparatus is as singular as we thought. Confession and absolution, love and fellowship, worship and thanksgiving, self-giving and intercession, even holy communion, come out to meet us in so many guises and in so many situations that we become bewildered. Is there any point in our continually acting out the patterns in our churches in quaint language and clothes and with quaint gestures, or do we simply content ourselves with naming the experiences as they occur to us in our daily lives? Or on the other hand, is it the acting out in church which helps us not to forget what seems in many ways an archaic mother-tongue? And even if it is, what is the connection between our interminable singing and mumbling, and our fairly unspontaneous behaviour in church, on the one hand, and God, creator and lover, on the other?

What, then, is the function of the Christian in the twentieth century world? First, I suggest, the courage and the willingness to learn how to hold opposites together in the mind until the "third thing," the new state of understanding, emerges. According to Jung "Life is born of the spark of opposites."

What form can this new life take? I suggest that the immediate and future value of the Christian may lie in the fact that, because of his awareness of God, he will have a stronger sense of identity than his non-Christian contemporaries. His "I" must become more firmly established than theirs, and therefore able to give them the kind of sounding they need if they are not to veer into mental chaos. "Love" nowadays, when it seeks a purpose within a Western society at least, should perhaps be turning away from social action, towards grappling with the problems of identity.

But if the Christian is to succeed in this, then his awareness of God must grow. In his need to discover "Who He?"—this God who is, and who is not—he will find himself plunging into a kind of mysticism that is both new and old.

And in order to bear this, he must do two costly things. One is to screw his faith much more tightly against his life, facing whatever sacrifices his integrity asks, in terms of giving up money, or success, or status, or, in some countries, enduring persecution and imprisonment. The other is to run right across the trend of our whole society, with its frantic emphasis on activity, and learn how to be instead of simply to do, learn how to sit still, and to face the stillness and occasional depression from which activity is an escape.

Being a Christian is a sort of dying. But it is the dying of the seed which falls into the ground, to be broken open in a new and unforeseen act of creation.

If men must cry, "The Church is dead," then we must shout, "Long live the Church!"

Forward Movement Miniature Books

25 cents per copy

A SHORT HISTORY OF THE
EPISCOPAL CHURCH,
by George Hodges, with an
Introduction and Conclusion
by Powel M. Dawley.

THE GOSPEL CONQUERS TIME,
by J. W. Hunkin.

GOD IN A TECHNOLOGICAL AGE,
by John Wren-Lewis.

THE BIBLE FOR TODAY,
by John Stirling,
in three books—
two on the Old Testament
and one on the New. Illustrated.